THE SAVVY COUPLE'S GUIDE TO
Marrying after 35

Kay Marshall Strom
& Daniel E. Kline

InterVarsity Press
Downers Grove, Illinois

InterVarsity Press
P.O. Box 1400, Downers Grove, IL 60515-1426
World Wide Web: www.ivpress.com
E-mail: mail@ivpress.com

InterVarsity Press® is the book-publishing division of InterVarsity Christian Fellowship/USA®, a student
movement active on campus at hundreds of universities, colleges and schools of nursing in the United States of
America, and a member movement of the International Fellowship of Evangelical Students. For information about
local and regional activities, write Public Relations Dept., InterVarsity Christian Fellowship/USA, 6400
Schroeder Rd., P.O. Box 7895, Madison, WI 53707-7895, or visit the IVCF website at <www.ivcf.org>.

All Scripture quotations, unless otherwise indicated, are taken from the Holy Bible, New International Version®.
NIV®. Copyright ©1973, 1978, 1984 by International Bible Society. Used by permission of Zondervan Publishing
House. All rights reserved.

Cover design: Cindy Kiple

Cover image: Steve Cole/Getty Images

ISBN 0-8308-2376-X

Printed in the United States of America ∞

Library of Congress Cataloging-in-Publication Data

Strom, Kay Marshall, 1943-
  The savvy couple's guide to marrying after 35 / Kay Marshall Strom and
Daniel E. Kline.
     p. cm.
Includes bibliographical references.
  ISBN 0-8308-2376-X (pbk.: alk. paper)
  1. Marriage—Religious aspects—Christianity. 2. Middle aged
persons—Religious life. 3. Spouses—Religious life. I. Kline, Dan,
1944- II. Title.
  BV4596.M3 .S78 2003
  248.8'44—dc21
                                                                    20022154308

| P | 18 | 17 | 16 | 15 | 14 | 13 | 12 | 11 | 10 | 9 | 8 | 7 | 6 | 5 | 4 | 3 | 2 | 1 |
| Y | 17 | 16 | 15 | 14 | 13 | 12 | 11 | 10 | 09 | 08 | 07 | 06 | 05 | 04 | 03 |

We lovingly dedicate this book to

Barbara and Al,

Jerry and Marian,

Paulette and Merrill,

Linda and Joe,

Lorayne and James,

Anne and Frank,

and all the other couples

who have helped us prove

that it is indeed far easier

to get happily married after 35

than to be hit by lightning.

Contents

Introduction

A nervous young groom with his blushing young bride all decked out in a flowing white gown and veil. Mother sniffling and Dad bidding farewell to his little girl. Piles of gifts—great stuff to fill a new home, however humble that first home might be. Plans for the day when there will be the patter of tiny feet running down the hallway. The beginning of a shared lifetime of ever-increasing prosperity, great career moves, and babies who will grow up and make their parents proud. That's our traditional picture of marriage.

But things are changing. People are waiting longer to get married. They see distinct advantages to remaining footloose for a while, to having time to set up a solo household, to traveling and having adventures before they settle down, to getting established in a career. In addition, as people live longer, healthier lives, travel widely and meet many more people, the possibilities of a remarriage burst through that original wedding photo. This might be because of divorce or it might be because of the death of a spouse. Today nervous young grooms and blushing young brides are being joined at the altar by just-as-nervous older grooms and radiant brides of many different ages.

We've all heard those miserable statistics about finding happy, successful marriage after *youth* has been replaced by *more mature*. Yes, even the one about a divorced woman over thirty-five having roughly the same chances of marrying again as of being taken hostage. And we're here to tell you we don't believe a word of it, not after the couples we have visited. Not after the stories we have heard and the things we have seen. Take a look at these facts:

- More and more people are choosing to wait until they are well into their thirties to even consider marriage.

- In a very unscientific but nonetheless telling study, in the year 2001 almost half the marriage licenses granted in Santa Barbara, our city of over 100,000, listed one or both partners as over the age of thirty-five. (Further inquiry showed us that Santa Barbara is not all that unique in this.)

- Even single people in their seventies and eighties see themselves with too much to give and too much they would like to receive to sit all alone for the rest of their lives.

- Mature men and women have the advantage of going into marriage with more realistic expectations, both of their spouses and of marriage in general, than do those just starting out in life.

But here's another fact—a more sobering one:

- Second marriages have an even greater failure rate than do first marriages.

> *This is one of the miracles of love,*
> *it gives . . . a power of seeing through its own*
> *enchantments and yet not being enchanted.*
>
> C. S. LEWIS, *A GRIEF OBSERVED*

We know something about both the challenges and the rewards of getting married after the age of thirty-five (way after!). Dan's first wife, Susan, died while he was in his late thirties, leaving him with twelve-year-old twins to raise alone. Two years later he married an older divorcée, a marriage that quickly succumbed to the challenges of not-sufficiently-considered second-time-around baggage. As for Kay, after twenty years of marriage she became the caregiver for her increasingly disabled husband, Larry. He died ten years later.

For more than a decade our families have known one another. We have been around to lend a helping hand and words of encouragement through our respective tough times. Over the years, the two of us went from acquaintances to friends to business partners, and in time our friendship blossomed into love. Now we are proud to be husband and wife.

Between us, we have chalked up fifty-seven years of marriage—and counting. During those years we have experienced life-threatening personal illness, long-term caregiving for two spouses with terminal diseases, the deaths of two spouses, divorce, single-parenthood, caregiving for previous parents-in-law, blending of family, reblending of family—in short, when we mention carting along baggage, we know what we're talking about. We have lived it. The luggage we carted into our marriage wasn't just in suitcases; it was in steamer trunks!

Yet this book is more than a collection of our experiences. We enlisted the assistance of seven marriage counselors, all of whom approach their work from a biblical perspective. Their help and advice have been invaluable.

You will also read the stories of ten couples, most of them presented as composites. This is because a survey we did drew from more than thirty-five couples from thirteen states, from California to New Jersey, Washington state to Florida. We felt that highlighting the pertinent points in fewer couples would be easier than asking readers to try to keep track of all seventy-four participants by name.

In age our total "population" runs the gamut from the mid-thirties to the late-eighties. Some had not been married before (including two women who were first married at forty-four); some had been divorced; and some had survived their spouses.

These couples come from different racial and cultural backgrounds, and various socioeconomic groups and ways of life. They met in different and sometimes surprising ways (including a dating service and via the Internet). The one thing they all have in common is that they were married after the age of thirty-five.

We are Christians, and it is our deep personal belief that all relationships are strongest when built on a primary relationship with Jesus Christ. However, we don't want to imply that Christian couples will always do well in their marriages while non-Christian or non-religious marriages are doomed to failure. Thus, the couples presented in this book have varied religious convictions. Some are Christian, some are Jewish and some are not particularly "religious" at all. It seems that a marriage is successful because a couple practices godly principles in their relationships, whether or not they are aware of it or explicitly intend to.

And that is the point of this book—to lay out in twelve chapters those godly principles that lead to success in the most intimate and important of all relationships: the marriage covenant.

Now, having said that, all the following people join us in assuring you, marriage is not just a fairy-tale dream for the young. You and your spouse truly can live happily *even* after!

Cast of Characters

These are composite couples created from our survey information.

Sophie and Russell *of California.*

They married in 1994, she at forty-four and previously unmarried. He is ten years older and has two grown daughters by a former marriage that ended in divorce. Sophie travels often as a graphic arts coordinator for a large retail chain, and Russell is an engineer, though he is now planning for his retirement.

Rebecca and Mark *of Kansas.*

They married in 1990. Rebecca was thirty-three and Mark was forty when they met in 1988. Rebecca had married for the first time in her teens, a marriage that lasted three years and produced one daughter. In addition to Mark's two older boys, who no longer live at home, they have one daughter of their own born in 1993. Mark is a property manager and Rebecca is an office administrative assistant.

Lillian and John *of Missouri/Guatemala.*

Married in 1996, both had been married before and lost their spouses to age and illness. Lillian was seventy and John was seventy-five when they decided to commit to one another. He had been a "flying missionary" based in Central America, and she was retired after forty years of teaching. Lillian has two children and three grandchildren, and John has three children and four grandchildren.

Maureen and James *of Texas.*

Maureen was thirty-nine when she married James, eight years her junior, in 1992. Neither having been married before, they now have three children of their own. She had come to faith years earlier, but James has avoided church because of unpleasant childhood experiences concerning his family's faith. Maureen teaches and works in health care, and James is a self-employed accountant.

Paula and Clifford *of California.*

Married in 1984, both had been married before. Paula went through a bitter divorce six years earlier, when her only son was fourteen. Cliff's wife died of cancer eight years earlier, leaving him with two preteen daughters. Neither intended to remarry, but after they met and fell in love, they changed their minds. Still, they decided to wait until their children were out of the house to join their lives permanently. Paula, who just turned sixty-five, is now a retired schoolteacher, and Clifford, sixty-six, is planning to retire from a career as a business owner.

Janet and Peter *of Massachusetts.*

Janet was thirty-six and Peter was forty when they married in 1979. Peter, a schoolteacher, had been a confirmed bachelor while Janet, also a teacher, had been previously married for ten years but with no children. After marrying they adopted a boy and a girl, now approaching adulthood. Janet came to Christ through the pain of her divorce. Peter, a nonbeliever when they met, was led to examine and then follow the Bible's teaching through Janet's solid and sincere conviction.

Andrea and Scott *of Michigan.*

Neither had been previously married when they recited their vows in 1999, she at thirty-five and he at forty-four. Deeply committed Christians, they make serving the Lord the central focus of their lives and marriage. Scott holds a management position in a family business, and Andrea is now a freelance editor and writer.

Nancy and Jeff *of Florida/North Dakota.*

Both come from prior marriages that ended in divorce. When they married in 1994, Nancy was thirty-nine and Jeff was forty-four. Both brought older children to the marriage, though none of the kids now live at home. Settling in Jeff's home state, Nancy works as an administrative assistant for a public agency, and Jeff is a salesman.

Diana and Greg *of Tennessee.*

This couple appears only in chapter eight, which deals with family blending. Diana was forty-four and long out of a bad first marriage when she met Greg, a forty-three-year-old man whose wife walked off one day, leaving him with their two young children. Married in 1998, Diana continues to work with churches on ministry and missions issues, while Greg builds a business as a self-employed architect.

Lynn and Anthony *of California.*

Neither had been in a prior marriage when they married in 1997, she at forty-one, he at thirty-six. They now have two young children and have relocated from the East Coast to California. Both have advanced degrees, and both teach at small private colleges, specializing in religious studies.

What Did You Expect?

Sheila was a college friend of Kay's. Actually, she was more like a college idol. Cute, blonde, perky—and engaged to Matt. What more could any coed want? Matt was tall, handsome and a star athlete. It didn't hurt that he also had lots of money to spend on his dates. Then, halfway through her senior year, Sheila did a shocking thing—she broke up with Matt. Rumors flew, but Sheila never explained herself. The only sensible explanation was that she had lost her mind. Why would anyone give up a catch like Matt? He could be anyone's "Mr. Right"!

Almost twenty years later Kay again ran into Sheila, who was just as cute and perky as ever, even with two little ones in tow. Sheila beamed when she introduced her husband of six years. His name was Wes, and believe it, he was no Matt. He was at least two inches shorter than Sheila and shaped like a bowling pin. To be perfectly honest, Wes was, well, downright homely.

Sheila! Kay thought. *What have you done?*

Over the next ten years, Sheila and Wes and their children drifted in and out of Kay's family's life. As Kay got to know Wes, she began to understand Sheila's decision. He was a truly loving and thoughtful husband, a wonderful fa-

What I wanted in marriage was a partner who really knew me, and who loved and respected me because of it. And that's exactly what I got in Wes.
SHEILA

QUESTION:
*What first attracted
you to your
significant other?*

ther and an all-around great guy. One time Sheila confided, "What I wanted in marriage was a partner who really knew me, and who loved and respected me because of it. And that's exactly what I got in Wes."

Is Sheila unusual to have passed over Matt in favor of Wes? We suspect, though Sheila never said, that she must have sat down one day and taken stock of her expectations of a marriage between herself and Matt, and found the imagined relationship lacking. If so, that would make Sheila unusual, even rare: to think through what she really wanted, to assess how realistic those desires were, and then to act on the decisions she was forced to face—all when she was barely in her twenties.

As we get older, as we "mature" into our thirties, forties, fifties and beyond, we are expected to act as Sheila did in her twenties—to become increasingly fair, objective and realistic. But do we? Are we? We all enter marriage with expectations—that is, needs and desires—most of them involving happiness, completeness, ever-growing financial security, perhaps a family. Yet how many of us have seen early "ideal marriages," say, between the beautiful cheerleader and the football hero or the class president and Miss "Most-Likely-to-Succeed," break down and fall apart some years later?

A beautiful face, a sexy car, a big-bucks job—these have been the bases of expectations for many newlyweds in our society. Whether that also helps to explain the drastic 43 percent divorce/separation rate—within fifteen years—among first marriages in the United States is hard to say, but the dissolutions themselves are a fact.[1] The same report further states that 33 percent of first marriages end within ten years, and 20 percent end within five years. Even more discouraging is this: according to this study and others, the sta-

---

[1]The Centers for Disease Control and Prevention, 1995 survey of 11,000 women, ages 15-44.

tistics are even worse for second and subsequent marriages.

This book is written for that somewhat older, "mature" audience: those of you who are thirty-five or more and are either contemplating marriage or wanting to ensure the marriage you are in is happy, fulfilling and a lifelong success. For those in the first category, whether or not it's your first wedding, or for those in the second category, whether married twenty-five years or twenty-five days, if you want the best marriage possible, you're going to have to do as Sheila did: start by examining your expectations.

You don't have to *lower* your expectations—Sheila didn't—but you do have to decide first if they are realistic, and second if they will make you truly happy and fulfilled. Once you've made these determinations, you may be surprised at just how well someone "unexpected" may fill the bill—including, for you married folk out there, that person you're already married to.

Much of the information in this book comes from our own surveys and interviews with couples over thirty-five, some married less than a year, but most ranging from five to twenty years and more. Additional information has been gleaned from other popular works on marriage and relationships. From our own data, two positive principal expectations emerged so clearly that we will assume these probably influence your own expectations, whether you are consciously aware of them or not. They can be defined this way:

- a desire for *unconditional* love

- a need for lifelong *companionship*

Truly unconditional love is possible only from God; no human being can sustain a love that is completely unconditional. But rather than a spouse with God-like powers, most of our respondents are actually expressing *a desire to be ac-*

I have seen more success in marriages after thirty-five—because there tends to be more individual maturity—though this is not always the case.

JOHN DEFOORE,
LICENSED MARRIAGE
AND FAMILY THERAPIST,
BOERNE, TEXAS

But God demonstrates his own love for us in this: While we were still sinners, Christ died for us.

ROMANS 5:8

cepted as they are, for who and what they are, and not judged on some subjective sliding scale. They don't want love to be given or withheld based on whether their behavior conforms to what a spouse decides is appropriate or inappropriate, pleasing or displeasing, approved or disapproved.

Companionship is harder to define in a sentence, but its essence seems to be *significant time spent with a best-friend spouse, usually engaged in activities that both partners enjoy and value.*

A successful marriage isn't finding the right person—it's being the right person.

Balancing these two rational expectations are two inter-related primary and unrealistic ones, bound to lead ultimately to dissatisfaction and a troubled relationship:

- an expectation that you can change your spouse (often to meet the next expectation)

- an expectation that there is a one-and-only perfect person out there meant for you and you alone

Our respondents seldom raised these issues, except occasionally as a "used-to-do," perhaps in a previous, failed relationship, or to talk about their futility. Yet time and again, these two "killer" expectations came up in literature and from marriage specialists who point out that either of these two prime problem-beliefs alone can doom an otherwise "good" relationship.

Therefore, in this chapter we will analyze the positive and negative sides of these attitudes and expectations, particularly in regard to love and companionship as well as "perfection" and an attempt to change the other person.

"Unconditional" Love

Perhaps 70 percent of our respondents used the term "unconditional love," and at least another 20 percent expressed the desire for and expectation of "true love," "lasting love," "real love" or some very similar term.

The first time Dan can remember using the term "unconditional love" was, oddly enough, at his father's funeral in 1992. He was giving his eulogy and was trying to be both honest and loving. There weren't many people present and those who were knew Dan's father well. He had a generous nature—in his own way—but a lot of his generosity was driven by a voracious need to be liked, loved and accepted in order to feel good about himself.

So when Dan said that his dad loved his family, he added, "But it was a conditional love, with everything for him quid-pro-quo—love on an 'if' and 'when' basis." On the other hand, Dan went on to say no one, no matter how pure the motives or how good the heart, can love another without putting some sort of conditions on that love.

In any event, the episode forced Dan to think about unconditional love. He's concluded that the closest human beings can come to what is otherwise God's exclusive province is to simply accept people as they are—and love them anyway. His parents would have had far fewer arguments if they had been able to do this, said Dan. "I can still recall one nasty fight that stopped suddenly when my dad yelled at my mom, 'If I wasn't good enough when you married me, why did you marry me in the first place?'"

His mother had no ready answer. But thinking about that now as their grown son, Dan believes she would have had to admit to her unrealistic expectations or to a belief that she could change his father for the better. And she, like many of us, was unprepared to do either.

We all want and need to be loved. It seems to rank right up there with food, water and air—a vital necessity. It's a major reason why we marry in the first place—"for love." But it would be best if you defined this term for yourself— what does it mean to *you* to be loved? And does the meaning

How do I love thee? Let me count the ways. I love thee to the depth and breadth and height my soul can reach.

Elizabeth
Barrett Browning

QUESTION:
What does it mean to you to be "loved"? And does the meaning change for you if the adverb unconditionally is placed before it?

change for you if the adverb *unconditionally* is placed before it? Take some time to think about this, then write out what "true love" from another person—your now or future spouse—would look like.

When it comes to loving, is there anything you need to do you aren't doing now? Is there anything you are currently doing that you need to stop doing? Anything you should be doing more of? Less of? Make some notes on what you can be doing to give "unconditional" love. Remember, the working definition of the term is *a desire to be accepted as I am, for who and what I am*, and not judged on some subjective sliding scale.

Past Experiences Set Up Present Expectations

There is no question that our life experiences can have a great deal to do with what we look for in a spouse, or if we even bother to look at all. Bad experiences can produce negative, avoidance responses and affect our ability to give or accept love. But not always, and not permanently—unless we let them.

Paula and Clifford had been married before, and both marriages had ended painfully, hers in a bitter divorce, his due to his wife's agonizing and protracted battle with cancer. But they found, like many others, that—with some adjusting of their attitudes and expectations—despite "experience" they could be happy in a new marriage.

We also talked to two women who had experienced very bad first marriages and were hesitant to try again. But their second husbands had never been married before and so they didn't feel the same concerns.

One of the women, a relative newlywed from California in her mid-thirties, said, "After a short, bad marriage which ended in divorce, I crawled into singledom not expecting to ever have a successful relationship with a man again. In counseling, I discovered that I didn't need to take all the blame for the failed marriage. I also found that just because I failed once didn't mean there was no one else who could ever make me happy, which is what I thought. So I made a mental list of what I needed and wanted in a relationship, and in many ways my fiancé didn't fit my list at all. Where I am hyper-organized and driven, he is laid back. Where I see the glass half-empty, he sees it half-full, and so on. Ultimately, I believe God gave him to me to teach me more about his unconditional love for me."

QUESTION:
Have you or your loved one had a bad relationship in the past? Does that pain still haunt you? What have you tried to do to break with those "ghosts" of the past? List your efforts below, along with any new ones you are now willing to try.

Paula and Clifford's first marriages each lasted about twenty years, and they have now been married to one another over eighteen years. They said, "After the sad and bitter experiences of our first marriages, neither of us wanted to go through that pain again. But God slowly changed our hearts and attitudes. After four years of friendship, shared experiences, thoughts and prayers, we decided we wanted to continue to be best friends, good companions and travel partners. We each wanted to serve the Lord and thought together would be more productive than separately. So we decided to share the challenges of life, for better or for worse."

The other of the two women from a bad first marriage, now in her late thirties and living in Indiana, has been remarried over six years: "Having come out of an extremely abusive relationship, my expectations were pretty simple. I expected that my daughter and I would be treated with respect, and that I would never have to seek protection from my new husband. I also came into this marriage with my own understanding that I had to love him *as he was*; that marriage should never be used as the 'springboard' to change him."

Both women are surprised—and very pleased—at how

QUESTION:
Write below the
source of past hurt
or anger and
how it got started.
Note the occasions
when you feel
those emotions.
What is going on at
the time to bring
them up again?
Most important,
how can you change
your perception of
the memory so it no
longer hurts or
angers you?

different their current marriages are from what they had originally imagined for themselves. The same is true for Clifford and Paula.

What about you and your significant other? Have either of you had bad experiences in past relationships? Does that past pain still influence any present or future happiness? If so, please understand that you can't change what's happened—that's all in the past. But you can change the way you think and feel about it. You can begin now breaking any hold the past still has on you.

Take a little time to start jotting down what those hurts are and where they came from. If anger is the more appropriate emotion, put down where the anger started and why it may still be affecting you. The healthiest thing a person can do is to let go of upsetting feelings. These can harm only the holder—you—and do nothing to affect the person(s) who may be the cause of them. If you're going to practice your unconditional love, keep in mind that forgiveness is a big part of it. (Sneak a peek at chapter ten for ideas.)

IT's NOT ALWAYS WHAT YOU MIGHT EXPECT

Not everyone we surveyed had to have bad initial experiences to be surprised at how different their "true love" was from their original expectation. This is what Peter—once a former confirmed bachelor in Massachusetts, now married over twenty years—had to say: "I was completely surprised that I was to be married at all! If I was to be married, after forty years of life, I expected to meet some buxom blonde about six feet tall with lots of money who would provide me with a life of ease. So much for fantasy. I got much, much better but in a slightly different package. Janet is a brunette, now a dazzling gray, five foot seven, and

I was earning more than she was when we met."

Russell, an introspective engineer originally from the East Coast who is now in his early sixties, has been married to irrepressibly independent Sophie for eight years. His viewpoint: "I didn't want to be alone. But I didn't have anyone like Sophie in mind, that's for sure. I came to California to recoup, for a time of reflection and of peace and quiet. After I met Sophie, that was gone. But actually, it was very stimulating to be with her, and we have adjusted to each other. It certainly enlarged my horizons. I had certain preset notions as to what I wanted in a wife, but then I met Sophie and they all disappeared."

Sophie, who was forty-four when she married Russell, had never been married before. She was as surprised as he was to find herself in love and wanting to marry. She says, "The qualities I looked for in a man when I was forty-four are not at all what I would have looked for when I was twenty-four. Before I met Russell, I had a list of seventy-two qualities a man must have in order to be worthy of me. I met Russell and he had three and I said, 'Close enough!'"

QUESTION:
What did you "expect" your significant other to be like? Did you have any preconceptions about looks, age, intelligence, personality, and so forth? How close to those preconceptions does your loved one actually come?

COMPANIONSHIP

Another frequently heard expectation was for *companionship*. The vast majority of our respondents stated right from the outset that what they looked for, longed for, needed just as much as love was intimate companionship. However, most were also wise enough to realize they could not expect their spouses to meet their every companionship need.

Here's what Rebecca and Mark, a Kansas couple married twelve years, have to say: "We both agree that our expectations were to share true companionship, where neither one of us was looking for someone to make us whole. We were both independent. We both had children. We both survived ugly marriages."

Nancy, a very youthful forty-seven-year-old from North Dakota, has this to say about her second marriage to Jeff, an extremely private and fairly opinionated man from Florida: "I expected that things would be perfect with a new and different husband. Wrong! Things were just as difficult in the relationship area. It was work with a capital W—just like before, only with less of the financial and none of the alcohol problems. I adjusted my expectations to a realistic level. I had to realize that he was not going to be my 'everything.' I still had to solve problems on my own, talk to girlfriends when I was upset—because as a man, he just couldn't understand some of that stuff."

Sophie had similar issues in adjusting her expectations of Russell's role as a companion.

> I had a best friend named Linda who listened to me when I had a problem. She sympathized and comforted me and said, "Oh, you poor thing! Poor baby!" Not Russell the engineer. He would just tell me the realities of how it is. So I went to a counselor and said, "Look at this! I talk to him when I have a problem and all he does is say, 'All right, here's the way it is . . .' Then I said, "When I go to Linda—" and the counselor stopped me right there and said, "You know what your big mistake was?" I waited. She said, "You should have married Linda!" Huh? Then she said, "Sophie, I know you. Listen to my advice: Stop trying to make him into a Linda. Linda's your best friend, that's what Linda is. Your husband is your husband. You're making a mistake to compare him with your girlfriend. He can't be all things to you. You're wrong and you're starting off on the wrong foot."

Good advice.

When Scott and Andrea married at forty-four and thirty-five, it was the first marriage for both. This is the way Andrea explains how Scott fills *her* need for companionship: "I feel I was more realistic in my expectations about married life than I would have been a decade ago. I love him more than life, and at the same time I don't expect him to fulfill every one of my needs for me. I have other significant relationships (women friends) to whom I can turn for support or encouragement. Although he is my favorite company, I don't need him to be around all the time, because I have learned to enjoy solitude."

Scott says, "I think, foremost, I expected love and companionship. By companionship I also mean sharing: new adventures, events like buying a home together, and most importantly building a family."

Maureen and James have different needs for companionship and they meet them in different ways. Maureen says, "I think it is very important to be realistic; no one person can fulfill all your needs. This was a lesson I needed to truly understand. I am a very social person, and James is not. I mostly and greatly wanted a life companion; I do not like spending that much time alone, such as living one's life alone without marriage. I like very much being married and having a partner, probably from being single for a long time."

James has a different take on the issue: "I expected that we would fulfill much of each other's desires for companionship. Maureen satisfies mine, but my needs for companionship and social time are far less than hers, so she wants more outlets. We had to come to an agreement that I could not happily fulfill all of her desires to go out and do things; she simply enjoys that sort of activity more than I do. That's meant she has enlarged her circle of friends and activities so that some don't include me. That works much better for us. I also had to let go of some expectations that we would enjoy doing the same types of things. Many times we agree that we'd like to spend

If a couple of weeks have gone by and you and your spouse haven't done anything together, it's time to get out of the house, even if it's just for a piece of pie at Denny's!

QUESTION:
*How would
you define
"companionship"
with your loved one?
How do you spend
time together?
What things do you
both enjoy doing?
Can you
comfortably spend
time together
without necessarily
doing the same
thing at the
same time?*

some time together, but we can't agree on how we'd both like to spend it. We're still working on that one."

What is *your* take on companionship? Do you look forward to spending time with your spouse or your intended? Take some time to list the activities you spend time on, including career, recreation and relaxation, sports, travel, church, and so on. Does your significant other share any of these interests? Would your spouse have a different list from yours? If so, how could the two of you spend more time together on the things you both value and enjoy? If there aren't many, how could you learn to enjoy sharing more activities with him or her?

Dr. Willard Harley, in his bestselling book *His Needs, Her Needs*, explains that in his extensive experience as a marriage counselor he has learned that a couple needs to spend about fifteen hours a week together, *actively* sharing a mutual interest. This averages two to three hours a day, every day. He also suggests that any couple work up to this amount of time because at first it will seem impossible to set aside that much time for each other every day. But with practice, it not only can be done, he says, but the payoffs are both enormous *and* gratifying.

THE VALUE AND IMPORTANCE OF FRIENDSHIP

Part and parcel of companionship was another element we'll call "best-friendship." To see the "whole person" means really getting to know them. That means becoming friends, real friends, and that almost certainly takes some time. This is another theme we heard again and again in both interviews and surveys—the importance of friendship to a married couple. Ideally, you are marrying or are already married to your best friend in all the world. That means you know them well, have seen their behavior under all sorts of conditions and circumstances, and still like them better than anyone else you know.

Here's what another woman we surveyed had to say about her husband of nine years: "Friends come and go; I wanted someone who would remain in my life year in and year out. I don't take marriage and my husband for granted. I try to savor each moment we have together, knowing what a good man he is."

One of the men in our survey had this to say about his wife of twelve years: "I wanted to marry my best friend, and she is my best friend. But I think I subconsciously expected that to mean she would be just like a guy. I had to learn just how much males and females are different (still learning). And not only can our interests be different, but our perspectives or approaches to our common interests can be different too."

And one of our "survey seniors," a man in his seventies, describes his wife of five years like this: "A loving companion, advocate, friend, pal, sweetheart, who is honest, truthful, candid, outspoken, knows what and why she believes or holds certain views and values."

We know how giddy and wonderful falling in love can be—we've been there too. And that's not to say that those feelings fade with time. No, instead they seem to mature into a different sort of love, one that is steady, constant and nurturing. Falling in love can be like a fire, which at first gives off intense heat. Staying in love is like the fire that then settles down to a warm, sustainable, gratifying glow (though it's always nice to know that anytime you add some extra fuel, it flares right up again!). It's like going from "friend" in the early stages, to "best friend" in the later stages, to "lover" when you first marry, to "lover *and* best friend" after you've been together for some time. Take it

There may be nothing more important in a marriage than the determination that it will persist.

DR. KINSEY, AFTER STUDYING 6,000 MARRIAGES AND 3,000 DIVORCES

HEART VERSUS HEAD:
Be realistic. Take at least enough time to really get to know your loved one. All of us have faults; can you live with your intended's and not plan on changing them "for the better"? This doesn't necessarily mean settling for "second-best"; rather, it may simply mean setting aside a demand for "perfection."

QUESTION:
Do you both have
an outlet for
emotional intimacy
in each other? Do
you take advantage
of it frequently?
What were the
circumstances when
you first had those
long, deep, personal
conversations?

from us and many, many other happy couples—the further along you go, the better it gets.

One of the first stages of falling in love is what psychologists call "verbal intimacy." Finding someone who listens sympathetically as we pour out our life story is both exciting and gratifying, and sooner or later this someone is bound to become at least a close friend. Most likely this happened at some point between the two of you; but the bigger question is, Do you both still have that outlet for emotional intimacy in each other? If so, do you take advantage of it frequently? What were the circumstances when you had those long, deep, personal conversations? Were you sharing a meal? Commuting together? Breaks at work?

If you haven't done so already, take the time and trouble to get to know—better—one another. Think about and list the fun times, and the deep, intimate, satisfying talks you used to have "back when." When your lists are ready, share and compare them with each other. Decide together which items on the list would give both of you the greatest satisfaction to do, to do more of, or to do again. Set aside at least one hour each week for this and other opportunities to go deeper into your friendship. Make sure the occasion gives plenty of room for talking—quietly, privately and without interruption or hurry.

FOR THOSE WHO ARE CONTEMPLATING MARRIAGE

The heart, the passion of the moment, can block the caution and reason of the head. It doesn't seem very romantic, but if you have doubts at times, or if your friends or family raise objections to your loved one, listen to those doubts or objections. Don't rush it; let these become part of the total assessment behind your commitment to this person.

Ask yourself, *Are my doubts or my friends' objections based on a lack of knowledge?* If so, you or your family and friends need to get to know your intended better. You can use the same techniques described above for married folks to learn more about him or her. The point is to use your greater maturity to be fair, objective and—above all—realistic.

As far as family and friends are concerned, remember Kay's comments about Sheila's husband Wes. As Kay got to know Wes, she found him to be a truly loving and thoughtful husband, a wonderful father and an all-around great guy. There's a pretty good chance your circle will come to see your intended in a similar light—once they get to really know him or her.

On the other hand, what if your doubts or their objections are reasonable? What if they are based on fact and observation rather than ignorance? If they correctly describe an integral part of your mate-to-be's nature, can you accept and live with that part of his or her personality?

Some of Dan's family and closest friends cautioned him about rushing the relationship that became his second marriage. It wasn't that they disliked or disapproved of the woman he'd fallen in love with, yet they saw things in her behavior and personality that they warned could portend serious incompatibilities later in the marriage. But, being deeply impassioned, Dan brushed off their objections—to his great regret when their concerns proved accurate. Mutual inability to compromise and resolve differences led to divorce within four years.

THE GREATEST FALLACY—CHANGING THE OTHER PERSON

The expectation that you can change the other person over time—or worse yet, that you have some sort of right to do

IDEA:
List below the fun times, and the deep, intimate, satisfying talks you used to have "back when." When ready, share and compare your lists with each other. Decide together which items on each list would give both of you the greatest satisfaction to do, to do more of, or to do again.

If any of you lacks
wisdom, he should
ask God, who gives
generously to all
without finding
fault, and it will be
given to him.

JAMES 1:5

Love is friendship
set to music.

E. JOSEPH COSSMAN

so—is perhaps the most unrealistic expectation of all—and maybe the most damaging as well. Your significant other is not only unlikely to change, he or she will very likely resent your attempts to make it happen, no matter how well founded or well intended. You will not only end up with an angry, disillusioned, resentful spouse—assuming the marriage takes place at all *and* holds together—you will probably also find yourself now put off by the very traits you once found so attractive and endearing.

Do these sound familiar?

She married him because he was so strong and manly. Now she says he's a "domineering male."

He married her because she was so cute and looked up to him. Now he says she is a helpless airhead.

She married him because he would be a good provider. Now she says he does nothing but work.

He married her because of the good, practical head on her shoulders. Now he says she is boring and no fun at all.

She married him because he was the fun-loving life of the party. Now she says he is nothing but a shiftless party boy.

What's so wrong with being manly, or cute, or dependable, or practical, or loads of fun? Nothing, unless either we see *just* that—what we want to see—or what the other person wants us to see, which again may be *just* that. It is only later, when we've been around for some time, that we start to see the other side of that once-attractive trait. And that's when we sometimes begin to think, *If I could just get him/her to _____ a little more (or a little less), things would be so much better for both of us.*

Psychologist-counselor Armando Quiros has this to say on the subject: "I don't believe in 'changing' the other person. For me this is about control. I apply the Alcoholics Anonymous prayer: 'Grant me the serenity to accept the things I cannot change (that is, the other), courage to change the things I can (me), and the wisdom to know the difference.' "

The great majority of the people we've interviewed say they anticipate and want to be accepted and loved for who and what they are, "and *please* don't try to change me!"

Russell has this insight into Sophie's personality: "My expectation was for companionship, but I took her on her terms because she is an independent, career-minded woman, and she is a success in that career. Changing each other is a lost cause. And I think once you recognize that, you can just enjoy each other."

But what about others who are already married and are now realizing that one or both partners have been trying to do exactly that—change the other? Well, take Russell's advice: it's a lost cause, and now's the time to stop. We would hope by now the lack of success would be proof enough that trying to change *another person externally* is futile. However, trying to change *oneself internally*, while usually very difficult, is not only possible, it is the only real avenue available to any of us.

Here is some more good professional advice, from Dr. Chérie Carter-Scott's bestselling book *If Life Is a Game, These Are the Rules.*[2] This little book is composed of ten short chapters, each explaining a basic rule. Here are some of our favorites, pertinent to any unrealistic, futile effort that we may make in life:

Rule Three—There Are No Mistakes, Only Lessons
Rule Four—A Lesson Is Repeated Until Learned
Rule Seven—Others Are Only Mirrors of You

> *I assumed my husband would accept me as I am. This was incredibly naive and unrealistic as he accepts nothing as it is. He is never satisfied to leave things or people as they are; he believes it is his duty to reform people and institutions.*
>
> A SURVEY RESPONDENT, MARRIED FIVE YEARS

---

[2]Chérie Carter-Scott, *If Life Is a Game, These Are the Rules: Ten Rules for Being Human* (New York: Broadway Books, 1998).

From Rule Four: "Does it seem as if you married or dated the same person several times in different bodies with different names? Have you run into the same type of boss over and over again? Do you find yourself having the same problem with many different coworkers?"

If the sweethearts, bosses and coworkers are all different, but the issues are always the same, then where does the basic problem most likely lie? What is the one factor common to all these situations? (Hint: check a mirror.)

There is a lesson to be learned here. We have no power or right to change another person, so don't even try. If the problem lies within, we have both the power and the responsibility to change ourselves. Resolve to start today.

MORE UNREALISTIC EXPECTATIONS

Now for the second great fallacy—that there is a "Mr. Right" or "Ms. Perfect" out there for you. This self-deluding belief has a couple of corollaries as well: One, this is the one-and-only person meant just for you and you alone. Two, the two of you will be instant soul mates.

*I am giddy,
expectation whirls
me around.*

SHAKESPEARE,
TWELFTH NIGHT

In fact, sociologists at Rutgers University National Marriage Project found that modern marriage is becoming more about the search for a soul mate than about raising a family. Sounds great, doesn't it? Someone who thinks like you, wants the same things you want, intuitively senses your needs and desires? Only problem is, it doesn't happen that way. Soul mates are made, not born. They develop over time. Expecting someone to intuitively understand you and know what you need and want is an exceedingly unrealistic expectation. This is something the two of us learned the hard way, even at our advanced ages and with all our experience in realism in marriage.

Having known one another for over eleven years by the

time we were married, we thought we were well aware of and sensitive to each other's needs. We didn't think we would have any really significant problems anticipating or meeting them. Wrong. It turned out once we were married we did expect—unrealistically—that if one or the other of us was feeling moody or hurt or insecure, the other would sense it and respond with an outpouring of love and care.

That did happen now and then. But as often as not, what was bothering one of us would sort of spill over onto the other, who would then misinterpret the reason behind the moodiness, or hurt, or insecurity. All too often one or the other of us would then react defensively, and whatever was wrong would be made worse, with the result that at least one of us would get into a snit and end up withdrawing from the other.

So now we're learning that we have to talk about what's wrong and get at the feelings behind the problem, and with no blame or guilt for where those feelings came from. We still find it difficult to do, but as we work at it we have begun to unlearn old patterns and reactions. We're starting to substitute more rational ones, responses based on talking, listening and assessing, all the while suppressing the urge to defend, to avoid, to hide out or stonewall.

This is what we mean when we say, "Soul mates are made, not born."

Equally unrealistic is the belief that there is just one perfect person for you. The myth goes something like this: If you find him or her, it was destiny, fate or the will of God— and if you don't, then you will have to settle for second- or third-best, or no one at all.

There is a huge problem with settling for a so-called second- or third-best person. You will either try to transform him or her into your version of an "ideal love"—that is, change the other instead of yourself—or you will often find

---

SIX KEYS TO A HAPPY MARRIAGE:
Out of seventeen components thought to form the bedrock of a successful marriage, these six were identified by more than nine out of ten men and women as "extremely" or "very" important:

- *Respect for each other*
- *Trust*
- *Honesty*
- *Communication*
- *Being good parents*
- *Having fun together*

REDBOOK MAGAZINE, 2001

*Unarmed truth and
unconditional love
will have the final
word in reality.*

MARTIN LUTHER
KING JR.

your spouse lacking and never truly commit yourself unconditionally. Some may argue that this amounts to "lowering
your standards."

We would say that if you expect "stupendous" all the
time, you are bound to be disappointed sooner or later. So
change your expectations from unrealistic to realistic, and
accept that you are marrying, or are married to, another human being, someone not unlike yourself, with problems, issues, hang-ups and habits. Then get ready to lay a solid
foundation together.

FOR DISCUSSION

Look at the following list. Do any of these "expectations"
sound familiar? They are stated in an extreme way, but
that's intentional; you can't miss the meaning. Check any
that apply, then start working to reverse them.

If you really don't believe you do any of these things,
check with your spouse. Ask for some objective feedback,
and be willing to do the same for him or her. If your spouse
or spouse-to-be feels that more than one item applies, to
minimize hurt feelings or defensive reactions, deal with just
one item at a time.

THE TEN DEMANDMENTS

- Thou shalt make me happy now and forever more.

- Thou shalt be who and what I want you to be.

- Thou shalt know what I need and want without my
  having to say a word.

- Thou shalt remember that it is more blessed to give
  than to receive.

- Thou shalt need no other friend than I.

- Thou shalt be the source of my self-worth.

- Thou shalt never fail to express gratitude for everything I do for you.

- Thou shalt never criticize me in any way, shape or form, or say or do anything to make me feel bad.

- Thou shalt overlook any mistakes I make and never bring them up to me.

- Thou shalt give me unconditional love, though I may withhold it from you.[3]

---

[3]John N. DeFoore, B.S., Th.M., and Marion Sue Jones, B.A., M.S.W., Consultant Services of Boerne, Texas, 1997.

Laying a
Sound Foundation

The average first marriage that ends in divorce lasts just eight years. For a second marriage, that figure drops to a dismal six years.[1] Pretty disappointing, even when you factor out that most of us get precious little marriage training in life—except for what we see at home. And for an awful lot of us, what we saw at home is pretty flimsy material. So we just get out there and do the best we can. And if that first marriage doesn't work out, we try again—and we make the same mistakes all over again. Only this time those mistakes are weighed down by all that left-over baggage we are lugging along from last time. As one fifty-eight-year-old divorcee says, "You may not know exactly what you want in a marriage, but you certainly know what you don't want!"

This may be the marriage you have been waiting for and planning toward for years. Or you may already be married, maybe for quite some time now. Either way, your chance of beating the depressing odds is far better if you begin by laying a firm foundation upon which to build a solid, healthy marriage.

---

[1]National Center for Health Statistics; Census Bureau.

So just what are the building blocks of such a foundation? Let's look at seven hefty ones that will go a long way toward supporting yours.

1. Do what makes each other happy.

2. Unpack your old baggage.

3. Build a friendship with each other.

4. Learn to communicate (really!).

5. Build a foundation of honesty.

6. Develop a healthy sexual relationship.

7. Forge an iron-clad union.

FOUNDATION STONE #1: DO WHAT MAKES EACH OTHER HAPPY

Obvious, you say? Something you started doing when you first looked at each other with interest in your eyes? Maybe so, but according to Dr. Willard Harley, in *His Needs, Her Needs*, it was when he started encouraging each spouse to do whatever it took to make the other happy and to avoid doing what made the other unhappy that the feeling of love between the two was restored. After years of frustration at seeing so many of the couples he counseled end up divorcing, he finally began to see marriages saved. "It is the feeling of love that's absolutely essential," Dr. Harley says. "In all my years as a marriage counselor, I've never counseled a couple in love who wanted a divorce."[2]

You started out in love. All you wanted to do was make each other happy. Here, then, is your cornerstone: Identify those things that make each other happiest and make them a regular part of your life.

Laugh together!
- *When something makes you laugh, invite your spouse to come and share in the fun.*
- *Look for a regular humor column in your newspaper and read it aloud to each other.*
- *When you're apart, call one another to share something funny that happened.*

---

[2]Willard F. Harley Jr., *His Needs, Her Needs: Building an Affair-Proof Marriage* (Grand Rapids, Mich.: Revell, 2001), p. 13.

QUESTION:
*What are three
things you know
will make your
spouse happy?*

Kay, for example, is not a morning person, although all her life she has had to function as one. Ever since she first married at twenty-two, she dutifully got up and prepared breakfast for everyone even though she was not the least bit hungry first thing in the morning. If she was under the weather, she brushed aside her own feelings and made sure everyone else was taken care of. Dan identified that love Kay has of snuggling down in the blankets and sleeping late, so he makes a point of nurturing it. Every morning he gets up first. When Kay awakens, by her bedside is the newspaper and a cup of made-from-scratch hot cocoa—bittersweet, just the way she likes it.

For one of our respondents, now in her eighties, happiness has taken on a whole new meaning since she met her new husband some years ago. "I honestly don't remember ever having laughed—I mean really laughed—before I met him. My parents never laughed, and so I never laughed. But he gets silly, and he just makes me laugh and laugh, and I really do love it!"

She even giggles when she tells about the first time they met: "I was driving past his office and there was a parking lot outside. Now, I'm not much of a driver, so I pulled over the curb and my car got stuck. I thought, *Oh, no, what am I going to do now?* So I climbed out of the car. He came out of his office and saw my predicament, and he suggested we call the auto club, which we did. Then he brought out two chairs and we sat down by the car and waited. And right away he started to make jokes! We laughed until the man came to check out the car. He simply lifted my car off the curb and I got in and drove away. I never laughed so hard in my life! That was ten years ago, and he is still making me laugh."

"Clifford is happy when he's on the go," says Paula of her nonstop sixty-six-year-old husband. "My biggest challenge is keeping up with him. He's involved with clubs and church meetings and fundraisers, and he loves to travel. Sometimes I just hit my limit. I have to say, 'Go on, I'm staying in tonight to catch my breath,' and he goes without me. We're both fine with that."

It's the opposite for Sophie, who is ten years younger than her sixty-two-year-old husband. "My energy level is still high, while Russell's is lower," she said. "At first I thought, *Why should I have to slow down just to accommodate him?* But once I decided, *If I want us to do things together, I do have to, that's just the way things are,* my attitude changed to one of looking for the benefits of slowing down rather than constantly being on the go. I've learned to see what it looks like being on the other side. I've learned to embrace a different kind of energy."

Pleasing each other. Laughing together. Fitting in with one another. These are wonderful ways of doing what makes each other happy. But there's one other element we must include here, and it's a scriptural principle too: affirmation. First Corinthians 8:1 tells us that love builds up. And we are reminded in Hebrews 3:13 to encourage each other daily.

Maureen, a Texan who at thirty-nine married a man eight years her junior—both for the first time—received these sage words from her new father-in-law: "Never, ever, bad-mouth your spouse to others. When you speak in public, build each other up." Pretty good advice on two points:

- build each other up

- in public

We can add one more: Be specific. We know your spouse has many, many wonderful points. And you probably have no trouble thinking of them on a moment's notice. But just in case, here is a list of fifty possible affirmations to get you started thinking:

But encourage one another daily, as long as it is called Today, so that none of you may be hardened by sin's deceitfulness.

HEBREWS 3:13

loving	imaginative	expressive	practical
energetic	caring	affectionate	calm
resourceful	loyal	organized	humorous
sensitive	fun	active	godly
sexy	exciting	forgiving	protective
cheerful	honest	adventurous	sweet
smart	committed	receptive	tender
decisive	attractive	reliable	best friend
elegant	interesting	responsible	flexible
thoughtful	supportive	dependable	wonderful parent
creative	thrifty	nurturing	understanding
gracious	funny	kind	
generous	considerate	gentle	

List your spouse's
top five best
characteristics:

1.

2.

3.

4.

5.

Doing things to make your spouse happy demonstrates that you have taken the time to get to know your spouse. And it really feels good when the person you love most cares enough about you to do that.

Kay loves the clothes from one particular outlet, but she felt they were too costly to buy for herself. So for her birthday last year Dan researched their catalog, discovered their website and ordered a dress for her ("It's my favorite," Kay says). In the process he also found that many of their items are sold at drastic discounts online. Now Kay has a fifty-dollar monthly allotment for the company's clothes, and she happily spends hours (and her allotment) each month reviewing the specials the company e-mails right to her computer.

Dan loves movies, especially those that deal with military history. But they are not always shown on television at convenient times, so Kay pooled her resources with her grown kids and together they bought Dan a DVD player for Christmas, along with some "starter" movie discs. She also got him a subscription to a DVD club and now he has a monthly allotment to spend on his movies. His collection has over twenty-five titles, and he gets to watch them whenever he wants. Sometimes Kay joins him, although war dramas are not her favorite video fare.

Dr. Harley says, "The husband and wife who commit themselves to meet each other's needs will lay a foundation for lifelong happiness in a marriage that is deeper and more satisfying than they ever dreamed possible."[3] Here's how King Solomon put it in Proverbs 15:15: *The cheerful heart has a continual feast.*

FOUNDATION STONE #2:
UNPACK YOUR OLD BAGGAGE

When Sophie met Russell, he was just coming out of a divorce after thirty years of marriage. At the time Sophie was a carefree forty-year-old businesswoman who had never been married and never intended to be. She had always lived alone, was in charge of her own life and loved having her freedom. Four years later they were married. "What a shock!" Sophie says. "Suddenly I realized my way wasn't the only way. I had to learn to back off and allow for a way of dealing with life that was very different from mine. That was not easy!"

Nor is it easy to unpack the baggage of old hurts.

"I've been through so much counseling," Janet says. "I know all about 'I statements' and 'active listening' and repeating back, 'What I hear you say is . . .' It all sounds great, but the problem is, it just doesn't work. When you're deep

When it comes to sex and affection, you can't have one without the other.

WILLARD HARLEY,
HIS NEEDS, HER NEEDS

Couples often ignore each other's emotional needs out of mindlessness, not malice.

JOHN M. GOTTMAN,
THE SEVEN PRINCIPLES FOR MAKING MARRIAGE WORK

---

[3]Ibid., p. 35.

in an argument, and you're feeling hurt and defensive, you just cannot talk or listen like a disinterested therapist tells you to. The bottom line is, my husband knows how to hurt me and I know how to hurt him."

Good point.

All our old sore spots are tucked away in that baggage. In order to change a stumbling block into a foundation stone, we need to unload it and quit carrying it around with us.

Both of us (Kay and Dan) have sore spots in our personalities, more than we like to acknowledge. One of Kay's is expecting to hear someone tell her, "You're a fat, lazy bum." Dan's is "You're no #$*% good!"

If these tender spots are pricked or poked, even innocently or inadvertently, we immediately become defensive. At first, we used to bump into each other's tender spots over and over. How could we help it? We didn't even know they existed. One time, during an argument, Kay said to Dan, "How come every time we have a problem you snarl at me, 'Oh, so you're saying I'm no #$*% good!' Why do you always do that?"

"I do?" Dan asked. It was news to him.

If something we said can be interpreted two ways, and one of the ways makes you sad or angry, we meant the other one.

Once we understood those tender spots, we were able to talk about them together. Now we know never to punch that spot. Even in our anger, we are protective of each other's tender areas. But we also understand our own hurts and we actually are able to laugh about them—although not when we are feeling vulnerable. What we are doing is unpacking and tossing out some old baggage.

Some tender spots are much harder to deal with. They are too deeply ingrained to be tossed away so easily. For Kay, indebtedness is a spot so tender that it almost brings her to the point of panic. The terrifying roots of financial insecurity go back to her early childhood. Yet debt is a fact of life for us right now. It is important that we both understand how hard this reality is for Kay so that we can work together on it in order to keep our sanity. It also helps us to handle our finances in a wise, realistic way.

For Dan, fear of failure is a super-tender spot. Like many people, Dan equates failing *at* something as *being* a failure. Intellectually, he knows this is false; he has even taught others to separate the two things. He also knows that failure in one area often means progress toward success in another. Despite all that, to be put in a position that might mean failing, or to hear feedback that to him focuses on a failure of his, just puts Dan in an angry, defensive, depressed sulk.

Kay knows that one of the keys to his dark moods is the way he talks to himself, how he interprets his own actions— or inaction—and runs them through a negative filter. So her goal is to get him to be more positive, to see himself as being part of God's loving plan. She has learned that when Dan is showing signs of feeling bad about himself, she can often help him out of his funk by urging him to read the Bible with her. He rarely turns her down. Although he's learned many ways to beat himself up emotionally, she also knows that he is almost always open to the Word of God. It is the one thing he would never dismiss as "pointless psycho-babble," the one thing that can always restore his sense of worth.

The baggage of questioning and doubting is not uncommon. "When you're young you tend to see things through rose-colored glasses," says Rebecca, forty-seven. "After eight years of marriage Mark went through a very sad and painful divorce. I married young, and after three years my husband walked out on me and our baby daughter. Both Mark and I were positive that we would never marry again, that we could never trust anyone again. We never even wanted to date. Yet here we are, married and committed."

Turning over my controlling tendencies to God is a real relief. Admitting I am powerless and that I need Jesus Christ puts my life in perspective.

JULIE M.

Mark adds this comment. "We met through a wrong number, believe it or not, and we communicated only by phone after that. For both of us, our biggest relationships had been with people who have serious psychological problems. It took us a long time to even get to where we were willing to meet face-to-face."

Working through such extreme baggage takes time. It's unrealistic to think otherwise. Certainly couples who have endured such great hurt would do well to seek the guidance of a qualified Christian counselor. Be aware that not all counselors are equal. We have heard scary accounts from people who have been given poor advice from counselors. Check their ideas with your own biblical and psychological framework. A qualified counselor can be an immense help. We, and many folks we know, can attest to that.

Lay a foundation stone of setting aside your baggage. Better yet, unpack the bag so that you can come to a better understanding of yourself. Allow your spouse to be a part of the process so that he or she can better understand you, too. Easy? No, of course not. It means making yourself vulnerable. But handled lovingly and carefully, that very vulnerability will bring you closer together.

FOUNDATION STONE #3:
BUILD A FRIENDSHIP WITH EACH OTHER

What does a marriage friendship look like? Like any other deep friendship, only more so. In a marriage friendship you will

- develop greater respect for one another

- rejoice with each other and celebrate each other's successes

---

There is a comfort in the strength of love; t'will make a thing endurable which else would overset the brain or break the heart.

WORDSWORTH

QUESTION: To what extent is your spouse also your friend? In what ways is your mate more than a friend? How can you keep loneliness from creeping into your marriage?

- understand the hurts your partner suffers and know how to help heal those hurts

- share your hopes and dreams, your ideas and viewpoints

- share those values you hold in common

- really, truly enjoy each other's company

John Gottman, in talking about happy marriages being based on a deep friendship, says that couples who successfully stayed married "tend to know each other intimately—well versed in each other's likes and dislikes, personality quirks, hopes, and dreams." That's a pretty good description of a friend, isn't it? In fact, after a fifteen-year study of over six hundred couples, Gottman concludes: "The determining factor in whether husbands or wives feel satisfied with their marriage is, by 70 percent, the couples' friendship."[4]

Again and again this is exactly the word couples we surveyed used to describe one another: "my best friend."

"My first marriage lasted almost twenty years," Paula said, "and I chose never to marry again. I would enjoy my own independent life and be as fulfilled as I chose to be—until Cliff came along. He taught me two could be one living under one roof and still be individuals and respectful of one another and allow each other their own space. I was very surprised and very happy. "Now we are best friends," she says of herself and her husband. "Together we are a team, and we will stick together."

Couples who are close friends are better able to bounce back after they are hit by crises. As the years pass, they will become closer and closer, with more and more in common.

Paula and Clifford have now been married two hundred

We love to travel together. We would never have done it alone.

JOHN AND LILLIAN

QUESTION:
How much time do you spend together each day
- *talking (and not just standard household stuff)?*
- *doing an activity you both enjoy?*
- *accomplishing something significant to you both?*
- *exercising or recreating?*
- *praying?*
- *meditating?*

---

[4]John M. Gottman, Ph.D., and Nan Silver, *The Seven Principles for Making Marriage Work* (New York: Three Rivers Press, 1999), p. 17.

and thirteen months. (That translates into almost eighteen years. Figuring that because they were both close to fifty when they married, they would probably not live long enough to celebrate fifty or seventy-five years of marriage, they decided to celebrate their month anniversaries.) "We pray together first thing before we even get out of bed," they report. "And more and more we choose areas where we can serve the Lord together. It has made a huge difference in our marriage."

Couples who are friends will be far more likely to give their marriage the one thing most couples say they crave: more time together. That is the thing many couples and counselors alike agree would make their marriages better. The better friends you are, the easier it will be for you to make the commitment to put other things aside, even important things, in order to give a priority to time together on a regular basis.

FOUNDATION STONE #4:
LEARN TO COMMUNICATE (REALLY!)

I tell male clients they should learn to set aside fifteen hours a week to give their wives undivided attention.

WILLARD HARLEY,
HIS NEEDS, HER NEEDS

Is there any couple who has gotten to this stage without being fully exposed to the importance of communication? Perhaps. But if either or both of you have been married before and have gone through marriage counseling, if you've taken any psychology courses, if you have read any pop psychology books, you know all about making "I" statements and active listening and so forth. You also know it works a whole lot better in theory than it does in real life.

Not long ago Dan made arrangements for us to have dinner on Friday night with our friend, Gerda. *But,* Kay made arrangements for us to have dinner the same night with her former father-in-law who was in town for the weekend. *But,* we weren't even going to be in town on Friday night. We were scheduled to be together in Los Angeles from Thursday through Sunday!

Are we just extremely poor communicators? No. But we do need something that most married-later couples need: a good dual method of organization and a committed resolve to use it.

The problem is, each partner comes into the marriage with an established way of life organization that has served quite well, thank you very much. For instance, Dan keeps his appointments on a management program on his computer. Kay has hers recorded on a calendar by her desk, carefully coded by ink color. Either of us can access the other's calendar fairly easily. Problem is, we don't. We just keep on dealing with things the way we always did in our previous lives. The result? Double-booked Friday nights and all the headaches and hurt feelings and finger-pointings that go with them. It isn't a question of the wrong way or the right way to keep track of dates. No, the real question is, *As we keep our own lives organized, how can we facilitate communication with each other?*

In this particular matter, we've decided to record everything that can possibly affect the other on a joint family calendar that hangs in the kitchen by the telephone. Now all we have to do is retrain ourselves to remember to do it consistently.

That's not to diminish the need for communication. It's vital. But perhaps it's time to take a step back to a more basic level of communication. Dr. Harley would call this simple conversation. In *His Needs, Her Needs* he writes, "The man who takes time to talk to a woman will have an inside track to her heart." He goes on to say that conversation not only communicates their needs to each other, but it teaches them how to meet each other's needs.

Communication, however, is even more about *listening*. Sometimes your partner simply wants you to hear what is being said. Other times, he or she is asking for some sort of accommodation, some small compromise that, if made, will bring greater contentment in the relationship. If you listen closely, you can pick up on this and offer to bend a little.

As an example, James said of his relationship with Maureen, "Some things have to be said repeatedly for them to be gotten across. Even then we're never sure about something we've said. What we think we said isn't necessarily what the other person thinks we said."

John Gottmann has identified several patterns of communication that he believes help determine which couples will stay happily married. Here are the positive communication techniques he believes such couples practice with their mates:

- They take turns talking.

- They refrain from giving unsolicited advice.

- They show genuine interest in what the other has to say.

- They communicate understanding of the spouse's problem.

- They take their spouse's side.

- They express a "we against others" attitude.

- They show their affections for each other.

- They validate their spouse's emotions.

Do you notice something about this list? Go back and underline those points that have to do with making yourself understood. Now circle the ones that focus on understanding your mate. Which do you have more of, underlines or circles? Here is the secret to successful communication: *First* and foremost, *focus on understanding the other person.* Making yourself understood comes in a distant second place.

If you really want to communicate with your spouse, it is vital that you look at the issue from the other person's side of the table. What you clearly see as a "six," your mate may be clearly seeing as a "nine."

"What I have learned in the years since Paula and I married is to listen better," said Clifford. "What I want to do is fix things for her. But I am learning to just listen. I don't have to make it better."

Yes. Just listen. And when you do share, keep the communication honest and current. As our friend and counselor Lynn Bunting tells us, "Speak the truth in love." How often we have taken that advice!

And while you are listening and speaking the truth in love, take care to share your goals and dreams with each other. Who better than the one you want to live it out with as you walk into the sunset?

FOUNDATION STONE #5:
BUILD A FOUNDATION OF HONESTY

Leo Tolstoy begins his great tragic novel *Anna Karenina* with this haunting line: "Happy families are all alike; every unhappy family is unhappy in its own way." Perhaps so, but the vast majority of unhappy families are alike in one important way. Almost all of them harbor secrets. And just about every marriage counselor in the world will tell you that honesty and the lack of secrets are at the root of really strong relationships.

The more years two people have lived before they came together, the more room there is for the gathering of secrets. So for those of us who marry at a more experienced age, the greater the danger of harboring those relationship secrets.

> *Most of "why things go wrong" and the anger and frustration that goes with it is due to a failure to understand one another. Understanding is based much more on hearing than on speaking, so if we want to improve on these communication breakdowns, it's the listening we need to work on, rather than the talking.*

"I expected that we would talk and that I would be able to be myself with Anthony," Lynn told us. "This was not something I had experienced with other men, as I was introverted and used to being alone. In the years between then and our marriage, despite physical separation and times when we were not communicating, I continued to see Anthony as my best friend, trite though that sounds. *But I am dismayed by how much of myself I continue to hide from him out of fear that he will condemn the real me.*"

One very important way to help build a foundation of honesty is to share your secret dreams, hopes and desires with each other. You need to risk letting the other in to that most private part of your life.

In 1984 Kay wrote a biography of John Newton, the eighteenth-century slave-ship captain who was converted to Jesus Christ. Although he is historically important for the part he played in the abolition of slavery, he is best known today as the author of the hymn *Amazing Grace*. Ever since, she has dreamed of writing a movie showing his swashbuckling exploits and using them to point to God's amazing grace. But she never dared share that dream with anyone. It was far too ridiculously fantastic.

Until Dan, Kay didn't share her John Newton movie dream with anyone. But when she did he was as excited about it as she was. He never doubted for a minute not only that the movie would be written but also that they would be sitting together watching the premier.

A poll by *Reader's Digest* magazine conducted in March 2001 stated that one in five people revealed that they cherished a secret dream they didn't talk about even with their spouse. "That result just blew me away," said Julie Gottman, wife of Dr. John Gottman. "Dreams reflect the deepest part of ourselves, and partners need to feel emotionally safe

Happily married couples largely succeed in avoiding these four negatives in their conversations:

- *Criticism*
- *Contempt*
- *Defensiveness*
- *Stonewalling*

JOHN M. GOTTMAN,
THE SEVEN PRINCIPLES
FOR MAKING
MARRIAGE WORK

enough to share them. This statistic tells us that one in five marriages are not safe havens."[5]

So sad. Lillian and her husband, the oldest respondents to our survey, had a great deal of insight and wisdom to offer. "Since I have been married to John I have learned to share very openly," she told us. "I talk to him as if I were talking to myself. It's a wonderful thing. I can say anything at all and he will accept it."

Talk. Let the other person get to know all of you—even that ugly part you would much prefer to keep hidden away or that secret part that makes you feel so vulnerable. But give each other a little space, too. The Gottmans insist that brutal honesty isn't always appropriate. You need to secure that foundation of closeness before you can start the really hard conversations. "When you have something yucky to talk about," says John Gottman, "it's better to start at a high emotional point than a low one."

FOUNDATION STONE #6: DEVELOP A HEALTHY SEXUAL RELATIONSHIP

"I was a bride at twenty, and my first husband was a year older," a thirty-six year-old from the Midwest told us. "I don't want to brag, but we were a pretty hot couple. We had our problems—we did divorce after seven years—but they were not in the sex department. Now I'm remarried to the greatest guy in the world, but let's face it, I'm not twenty anymore. And to tell you the truth, I'm afraid a great sexual relationship is a thing of the past."

Interesting thing about sex: so much of it depends on our attitudes and mindsets. Many older couples are convinced that sex will have to be different simply because they are no

I am dismayed by how much of myself I continue to hide from him out of fear that he will condemn the real me.

LYNN, MARRIED TO ANTHONY FIVE YEARS

If I ask, "What's wrong," and you say, "Nothing," I will act like nothing's wrong.

---

[5]*Reader's Digest*, LPV, August 2001, p. 83.

longer in their twenties or thirties. Then again, others see another kind of change in store for them.

"My mother told my sister and me that sex was a duty we owed our husbands, something we would just have to grit our teeth and endure," said a fifty-something women from New Jersey. "I always considered it dirty and nasty, something to be avoided if possible. After my divorce, I went a bit wild. I'm not proud of those days, but I do wish I had known when I was first married what I know now. I find so much more enjoyment in my sexuality in my second marriage."

Several women commented that they never were able to develop a healthy attitude toward sex. This was especially true for those who married young. That's distressing, because without a full and healthy sexual relationship, the entire foundation of a marriage can be weakened.

Marriage and family counselor Armando Quiros says, "Being physically, sexually intimate often is one of the important foundation stones of a healthy marriage relationship, whether or not that includes full-on intercourse."

Willard Harley gives two steps for achieving sexual compatibility:

- *Overcome your sexual ignorance*. A husband and wife must each understand their own sexuality and their own sexual responses.

- *Communicate your sexual understanding to each other*. A husband and wife must learn how to share what they have learned about their own sexual pleasure and fulfillment together.[6]

These are excellent building blocks for couples who have been married before and may be tempted to compare

The husband should not deprive his wife of sexual intimacy . . . nor should the wife deprive her husband.

1 CORINTHIANS 7:3
(NLT)

---

[6]Harley, *His Needs, Her Needs*, p. 53.

their new partner and relationship to the former one (either positively or negatively!). They're also for those who have never been married and fear their inexperience with a marriage partner.

A part of overcoming sexual ignorance is discovering to what degree your age and specific circumstances truly do impact your sexuality. All of us savvy couples are over thirty-five. Some of us are *way* over thirty-five. (Interestingly, our oldest respondents—in their eighties—were among the few who referred directly to their own sexuality!) And in addition, some have physical problems. So how does the marching on of time really and truly affect this foundation stone of a new marriage?

For some of you, regardless of your age, sex with your spouse may be exciting, energetic, joyful and mutually satisfying. For others, it definitely is not.

"We didn't marry for sex," a grandmother of eight told us. "Not at our age. We wanted a deep companionship, a real connection between us, a steadfast partner."

Certainly the things she talks about become more and more important with increasing age. But they can be heightened by the deeper sharing and tender playfulness that Lillian and John tell us belong to the mature lover. "Nothing is as affirming as that," Lillian said. She refers to it as "renewing love."

Couples who marry at a more mature age are able to not only rejoice in one another sexually, but at the same time to nurture and affirm each other. It is true that our bodies do not continue to respond the same way indefinitely. Arousal may not occur as spontaneously. A man may need greater sensitivity and patience to get and keep an erection. A woman may need stimulation over a longer period of time. Yet even these adaptations can bring about greater tenderness and a deeper sense of connection. But why would a loving couple complain about lying intimately together for a longer time, anyway?

And although many men may disagree, it *is* okay if all lovemaking doesn't end in the husband's climax. Yes, that may be a man's greatest physical pleasure in making love, and yes, to many men it's the greatest evidence of a man's virility. But if he doesn't, or can't, always ejaculate, does that have to mean his lovemaking has no point? Not at all. Even without it, lovemaking can be wonderfully satisfying. What about the enormous pleasure to be gained simply from exploring, kissing and stroking his wife's delectable body? What about the pleasure they will both get from playful sex games they can invent together, or massaging or caressing one another, or bathing or cuddling together?

Here is a rule of married life that we all recognize as wise—until we need to apply it personally: *Don't worry about your actual sexual performance.*

The surest way to become psychologically impotent is to worry about achieving an erection rather than simply allowing yourself to relax and enjoy the moment. It is extremely easy to psych yourself out. And to assume the worst of your partner.

"I hated to get undressed on our wedding night," Sophie said. "I was forty-four years old. Believe me, I didn't look like a model. I just knew he was going to jump in the car and drive away the moment he saw me."

We are victims of our culture. We are also victimized by reminders of our mortality. We need only look in our mirrors to be reminded of that. Kay has this to say: "The greatest wedding gift Dan gave me was to tell me—and demonstrate to me—how much he likes my body. I mumble apologies for all the wrinkles and lumps and flab, and he treats me as

Tell your spouse three things you truly enjoy about his or her physical appearance. Listen appreciatively, without disagreeing, as your spouse tells you three things he or she enjoys about you physically.

though all those were just beauty marks. He honestly seems to like the way I look! Amazing!"

Dan says this: "Kay has an inherent sexiness that is really very attractive to me. It isn't coyness or flirtatiousness; it's just something in her basic nature, and it will always be there. It's illustrated in part by the pleasure she gets from long, fragrant bubble baths, or wearing silky nightgowns to bed, or choosing lingerie by style and feel rather than cost or practicality.

"She grooms and dresses herself to suit her own taste, yet the effect is as though she's done it to please me. I can't imagine her ever schlepping around the house in an old robe and tattered pajamas, or coming to bed with her hair in curlers and night cream smeared all over her face—it's just not her."

To come to where you can enjoy one another's sexiness irrespective of physical traits is a wonderful quest. You may even find that those physical imperfections become marks of beauty in your eyes. Being sexually alive and intimate, bringing each other true pleasure, will do that.

Adventure, excitement, great pleasure. We don't abandon our rights to those things as we mature. On the contrary, we enrich them. We give them a deeper meaning.

For this reason a man will leave his father and mother and will be united to his wife, and they will become one flesh.

GENESIS 2:24

FOUNDATION STONE #7:
FORGE AN IRON-CLAD UNION

Sophie writes: "I used to eat on the run a lot. Now I am home almost every night, and Russell and I cook dinner together. When I was single I would spend three or four nights a week with friends. I spent my time however I liked, and I didn't have to check with anyone or consider anyone else. Getting married has meant a lot less time with friends. Now the two of us choose to spend our time together."

Another woman, also married at forty-four, said, "My husband and I are not bonded at the hip like we might have been if we were younger when we married. He has things he does on his own and I have things I do on my own. I think that's healthy for us. We give each other space."

On the other hand, Clifford and Paula emphasize the importance of being a team, of being a couple against the world.

Where you go I will go, and where you stay I will stay. Your people will be my people and your God my God.

RUTH 1:16

Who is right? All three, says counselor Armando Quiros. In fact, he sees them as pointing out three facets of the same togetherness stone:

- Together: Spend enough time together in whatever way is mutually satisfying. When you are together share and listen empathetically.

- Separateness: Acknowledge and respect it. Promote it in the other as well as in yourself.

- Union: Your goal is to *complete*, not to *compete*.

We cannot say which approach is right or best for you. All we can say is that it has to be comfortable and workable for both. If he enjoys a golf game every weekend but she resents his absence, or she has committee meetings every week while he stays home and sulks, then your marriage is headed for trouble. On the other hand, if you spend so much time together that at least one of you feels smothered, that too can lead to problems.

Keep in mind that the togetherness stone does have three sides, and the point is to seek balance in all of them. Communicate with your partner if you feel your relationship is getting out of balance somewhere. And remember that all communication is based on listening, understanding, effort and patience.

THE PERFECT MR(S). RIGHT

An incredible love-after-thirty-five story occurred half a century ago in the unlikely person of a brilliant, if somewhat stodgy, confirmed bachelor of fifty-eight by the name of C. S. Lewis. An unconventional American poet, Joy Davidman, interjected herself in his life, and the two formed a friendship that seemed to puzzle and bemuse everyone who knew them. Out of pity for both her emotional and physical condition—she was suffering from terminal cancer, and Lewis didn't want her to die alone in a hospital—he offered to marry her so he could care for her and her young son honorably in his home. But two unexpected things happened: Joy's cancer went into remission, and Lewis plunged head-over-heels in love. Years earlier he had written a spiritual autobiography titled *Surprised by Joy,* and now suddenly—ironically—he was surprised by Joy all over again. They had only four years together, but those years were marked by passion, excitement and gratitude for knowing a love he never thought was possible.

If we had never fallen in love we should have nonetheless been always together, and created a scandal.

C. S. LEWIS,
A GRIEF OBSERVED

Every marriage is a union between two people who bring to it their own opinions, personality quirks, background experiences and values. The longer the two have lived before they come together, the more profound and deeply ingrained these elements will be. Perhaps some of you are reading this book precisely for the purpose of learning how to deal with a difficult person. (Did you ever pause to consider that you might be someone else's "difficult person"? Scary thought, isn't it?)

Russell wrote, "When you are 24, you tend to wonder, *Is there a better woman out there for me? When* you're 54 you quit thinking that way. My experience told me that this time around, I picked a good woman."

Ready to turn some
of those flaws into
strengths?

Flaw:

Strength:

Flaw:

Strength:

Flaw:

Strength:

Flaw:

Strength:

Flaw:

Strength:

Flaw:

Strength:

You both have strengths and you both have weaknesses. You both have secure areas, and you both have places of great vulnerability. Allow each other to see all of it—the good, the bad and the ugly.

If you think you have found the perfect mate, you are in for a terrible shock. If you think you will take the raw material before you and *make* it into the perfect mate, you are in for an even bigger shock. Remember those expectations in chapter one? You are not going to find perfection in your mate, nor is your mate going to find perfection in you. Instead, look for a way to blend your strengths and weaknesses. Learn the wisdom of compromise.

Want to make your foundation not only secure but beautiful as well? Then practice the art of turning your loved one's flaws into strengths. Here's what we mean:

Flaw: "He is so stubborn!"

Strength: *"It's so great to be with someone who has the courage of his convictions."*

Flaw: "She is so quiet and withdrawn."

Strength: *"It's great to be with a woman who thinks things through rather than just jumping to a conclusion."*

Flaw: "He never tells me he loves me."

Strength: *"It's wonderful to have someone show me his love in so many ways."*

Flaw: "I used to have so much independence."

Strength: *"It is so great to have someone to come home to."*

FOR DISCUSSION

How firm is your foundation? Take a moment to think about the following questions and circle your response.

How often do you

do something solely to make your partner happy?	*Often*	*Sometimes*	*Seldom*
build him or her up in public?	*Often*	*Sometimes*	*Seldom*
express the things you most admire in him or her?	*Often*	*Sometimes*	*Seldom*
share your fears with your spouse?	*Often*	*Sometimes*	*Seldom*
set aside time to spend together every day?	*Often*	*Sometimes*	*Seldom*
regularly share your dreams, ideas and viewpoints?	*Often*	*Sometimes*	*Seldom*
truly enjoy each other's company?	*Often*	*Sometimes*	*Seldom*
try to understand what your spouse is saying to you?	*Often*	*Sometimes*	*Seldom*
take each other's side?	*Often*	*Sometimes*	*Seldom*
discuss what gives you sexual pleasure?	*Often*	*Sometimes*	*Seldom*
feel comfortable with your level of togetherness?	*Often*	*Sometimes*	*Seldom*
enjoy the feel of your spouse's body?	*Often*	*Sometimes*	*Seldom*
experience tears of joy with your spouse?	*Often*	*Sometimes*	*Seldom*
feel touched by his or her vulnerability?	*Often*	*Sometimes*	*Seldom*
feel connected to your spouse from a distance?	*Often*	*Sometimes*	*Seldom*
appreciate that your spouse is in your life?	*Often*	*Sometimes*	*Seldom*

If you answered "often" to the majority of these questions, you probably have a deep connection to your spouse. But if you had to think about your answers or scan your memory for the last occurrence, you may still have something important to learn about meaningful contact. You cannot deepen your love without connection. It's never too late to learn how to do it.

3

Money,
the Root of All . . .

James, an economist by training, was raised in a financially conservative household. So was his wife, Maureen. That's where the similarity between them ends.

> She and I have different approaches to money and spending. Maureen doesn't like to balance her checkbook, not ever. She's happy to have just a rough idea of the balance. I like to have my bills planned out for the month and know that the money will be in my accounts to cover them. Now that I do freelance work at home when I can, my income varies greatly, so I do even more planning. I get aggravated when, at the end of the month, bills are due and Maureen says, "Sorry, I won't have my share of the mortgage until a few days late. But it's okay, we have a grace period." I've never believed in using grace periods on bills, especially important ones.

As soon as you start talking about finances, Maureen starts sighing. "When I was a child, I didn't have many clothes," she says sadly. "Mostly I wore hand-me-downs. How I longed to be a pretty woman with nice clothes! I wanted to be able to buy whatever I wanted. And, since I was single until I was thirty-nine, and I was living on my

I found it an adjustment to have to think before every purchase of clothing or book—will Lynn think I'm being extravagant? Will my buying this mean that she can't buy something she needs?

ANTHONY

O, money, money, money, I'm not necessarily one of those who think thee holy, but I often stop to wonder how thou canst go out so fast when thou comest in so slowly.

OGDEN NASH

QUESTION:
How would you describe your financial philosophy? How about your spouse's?

nurse's salary, I was able to do it within reason."

That's when she shoots a meaningful glance in James's direction.

"I don't like to make many impulse purchases," James explains. "I rarely buy new things to replace old ones if the old ones are still serviceable. I buy things I want, but only after careful consideration of how much I really want them and whether I will still think them worthwhile after I've had them a while. I don't mind wearing old clothes in the least."

So who's right, James or Maureen?

Maureen, you say—within reason? Outside of reason, you think maybe James? Or would you vote the other way around? And anyway, just where is that line of reason?

That's the rub in any difference of financial philosophy, isn't it? Finding that middle ground. That evasive point that makes sense to everyone.

Commenting on Ronald and Nancy Reagan's fiftieth wedding anniversary, Dr. Joyce Brothers said, "That's an incredible amount of time for a second marriage. Second marriages statistically have a less likely chance of making it forever. The main reasons are money and kids."[1]

Let's look at the money. (We'll look at the kids later.)

TWO PEOPLE, TWO IDEAS

One of you wants to save for a rainy day; the other wants to live for today, enjoying life while you can. One wants to buy only what you can pay for with cash—or at the very most what can be paid off at the end of every month; the other believes that living off credit cards is the acceptable American way.

One believes each partner in a marriage should account

---

[1]Dr. Joyce Brothers, quoted in an article by Jeff Wilson for the *Santa Barbara News Press*, March 4, 2002, p. A3.

to the other for any and all expenditures; the other believes only major spending needs to be shared with one another—if any at all.

Who's right? No one is. Both of you are.

These are not wrong/right sorts of questions. They are how-can-we-work-it-out-so-that-it's-right-for-us? sorts of questions, and there is a huge difference between the two. That's because what works perfectly well for one couple would be absolutely unacceptable to another. Our way may not be your way. The only reason the couples we cite here are important to you—besides just for interest's sake—is the way in which their stories might help guide you to find the best path for you and your spouse or spouse-to-be.

DISCUSSING YOUR FINANCIAL PHILOSOPHIES

Believe it or not, many people over thirty-five go into marriage not knowing the extent of their spouse's assets and debts. It seems obvious that making full financial disclosures to each other would help form a foundation for a healthy, lasting marriage—even if the financial news is bad. Those credit card debts are sure to surface sooner or later.

When you are joining your lives together, there is much to consider:

- bank accounts

- retirement accounts

- property

- life insurance policies

- wills and trusts

- short- and long-term debts

What if you had a choice between a loveless marriage and extreme wealth, and a loving marriage and a lifetime of poverty? If you are like nine out of ten men and women, you'd choose to be poor but happy.

REDBOOK MAGAZINE SURVEY, 2001

For many people, financial assets are the result of years of hard work, careful saving, frugal living and bequests from loved ones. No wonder it's hard for them to loosen their grip—even for a new spouse. And yet misunderstandings, suspicion, confusion and hurt feelings often result from the reluctance to share. Patience is clearly needed, as well as a careful explanation of the motives behind our actions and feelings—probably a number of times.

My bounty is as boundless as the sea, My love as deep; the more I give to thee, the more I have.

SHAKESPEARE

"Wanting to hold back must mean he doesn't really love me!" a new wife may say of a husband who balks at changing the life insurance beneficiary from his children's names to hers. But the husband might explain: "I'm concerned about the children's education. That's why I took out the big policy in the first place. Once they are through school, I'll gladly make you the beneficiary."

"Obviously she isn't sure she really wants to make this commitment," a new husband may conclude when his wife declines to put ownership of the family house in his name as well. The wife may have an entirely different explanation: "My first husband's parents gave us the down payment, and we worked and saved to pay it off with the intention that the house would someday go to our children. I need to honor that. We can blend everything else, but we need to put the house in trust for my kids."

Andrea understands how hurt feelings and suspicion can develop. "It bothered me a lot that Scott kept his mother's name on his bank account after we were married rather than immediately changing it to my name." But then she adds, "To his credit he fixed this situation when he realized how important it was to me. That was the moment I felt we were really married, without any safety net."

Love, commitment and trust may well have nothing to do with these decisions. It may be something—or someone— else entirely.

For Mark and Rebecca, the hang-up was her father. "Rebecca grew up rich and I grew up poor," Mark explains. "And her wealthy, overbearing father put great financial pressures on us. I was expected to provide for her 'in the manner to which she had become accustomed'—thanks to her dad.

"My expectation was we would have to scrimp and save to, first of all, get ourselves into a bigger house for ourselves and the kids. But at first, Rebecca would spend freely on our credit cards whenever she wanted something, and then she wouldn't tell me about it until after the bill arrived in the mail. This caused us lots of problems until we finally sat down and talked about our different feelings about money and debt. It was really hard at first, especially for both of us not to think 'I'm right and you're wrong.' But eventually we came to an understanding about how we'd spend and save our money and we haven't had too many problems since."

For another young newlywed couple, it was expectations from their pasts that caused the most trouble. "My parents— and my first husband—believed that couples' finances should be joined," the wife told us. "There should be one checking account, joint credit cards and full disclosure in all financial matters. His parents had kept their money separate—they were almost secretive about it. So we had opposite models. Finances are still the biggest stickler for us."

Her husband agrees. "Up until our marriage I had been very independent about my money," he says. "Now I have to discuss my spending first and get her okay. Sometimes she doesn't agree that we—or I—really need what I want to buy, and I don't always give in easily when that happens. So I'm still having some trouble with giving up that independence."

Their situation is compounded by the fact that they are paid differently. She gets paid monthly, while he is paid weekly. They have developed a system where she pays all the bills, but he gives her a weekly amount to deposit and then keeps the rest to use as he pleases. "He often uses it for little gifts for me or fun activities for us together," she adds.

We were actually quite surprised to see that close to two-thirds of the couples who responded to our survey had opted to keep their finances separate, a percentage we wouldn't have expected.

Sophie and Russell each have their own checking account, then they have a joint account which covers such things as house expenses and vacations. "Many of my friends told me this was a big mistake," Sophie says. "They said as soon as they got married their husbands took over the finances. I said, 'No way! Not me!' I had been on my own too long. Fortunately, Russell agreed and it has worked out beautifully."

TALK, TALK, TALK

Frank discussion is the first and most obvious step in working out finances. Yet, amazingly, many couples stumble along trying to avoid it. They struggle, they bicker, they battle . . . and too often money issues kill their relationship. National statistics show that as many as 70 percent of divorcing couples attribute the breakdown of their marriages to arguments over finances.

Whether or not that statistic is valid, right here is the key to resolving your money battles: talk, talk, talk, and talk some more. Talk about your financial philosophy. Talk about your financial goals. Talk about your financial fears.

Mark and Rebecca finally got their differences resolved when they talked it out, and both wish they had done so sooner, even *before* they married. Sophie and Russell worked out early in their marriage how they would set up separate and joint accounts for both personal and mutual uses. And Andrea and Scott resolved how their joint accounts would be held, with Scott deferring to Andrea when he realized how important the issue was to her.

Many of our newlyweds could echo Andrea when she said, "Finances are still the biggest stickler for us." She and Scott are on their way to working matters out, but they still have quite a way to go before both of them will feel completely at ease with their arrangement—whatever it ends up being. Their experience underlines our point: best if these financial matters are fully discussed long before two people actually tie the knot.

There is no getting around the fact that some situations are difficult to resolve. No matter what is done, some cases simply prove the adage that "you can't please everyone" regardless of what you do. For example, a man who is divorced is often paying alimony to his first wife and child support for their children. In effect he is helping support two households.

"You pay them too much!" his new wife may insist when she looks with dismay at their own mounting bills. "Tell her she will just have to do with less."

It is up to the man to tell his new wife that no matter how much they are struggling, that first family is also his responsibility—both morally and legally—and he will honor his responsibility as an adult and parent. The new wife may not agree, and she certainly won't like it, but there is really no other option—she will have to learn to live within a budget dictated by both past and current obligations. She may even have to take a job to help her husband support the first family.

And, of course, this is the very sort of thing that is always best discussed before marriage so that both partners-to-be know exactly what they are getting themselves into and are in agreement about how they will deal with it. If you are already married and you and your spouse still face unresolved financial problems, set a date to sit down and get busy talking about it. Remember: patience is vital. You may well have to say everything five or ten times before being understood and acknowledged—and even then you may not get agreement!

For Sophie, like others, talking about finances has been the greatest challenge of her marriage. "I've always considered myself to be good with money," she says. "Being single until I was forty-four, I never had any debt other than my mortgage or car payment. On the other hand, I've never kept track of how I spent my money, either. Russell, however, is a planner and has always lived on a budget. I've resisted this idea for years, and at times I'm fearful he will force me to change. When I feel threatened I get angry and tense. We are definitely getting better at talking about money—particularly about living on a budget. It has helped tremendously that at heart our philosophy toward money is similar."

Russell, ten years older than Sophie, wants to retire this year. That means they will need to be more budget conscious than ever. "We've been talking about this for years," Sophie says, "and I've agreed that he needs to retire. I've mentally adjusted to living on more of a budget."

After you've talked it out, build a plan together. Yes, you may need a budget even though you never did before. And yes, you may need more accountability than you like. But, hey, you're a partnership now. It's a whole new world.

You say all the talking in the world isn't going to get you where you need to be? You say your issues are just too great? Or that every talk ends up in an argument? If that's the case, it may be time to look into financial counseling. There are books available to get you started, and if that isn't enough, there are actual financial counselors with whom you can sit

Birth parents are responsible for their children regardless of who else comes along.

NANCY AND BILL PALMER,
THE FAMILY PUZZLE

down and work out your own particular situation. This makes a whole lot of sense when you consider Dr. Brothers' dire pronouncement of the havoc money problems can play on a later marriage.

PRENUPTIAL AGREEMENTS OR JUST A WILL?

Another thing that surprised us was that more than a few couples had actually pursued a prenuptial agreement of some kind. More and more mature couples who have built up assets of their own, it seems, are looking to such agreements as something that is actually in everyone's best interest. For starters, these agreements stimulate communication about finances. And once the door is open to the difficult subject of money, it's a lot easier for the two of them to talk about other difficult subjects.

One about-to-be-married woman who would bring nothing tangible into the marriage suggested a prenuptial agreement to her intended, who had an expensive home and a hefty portfolio of stocks and bonds. He declined. "Why start off a marriage planning for its possible failure?" he asked.

Actually, say proponents, a prenup increases the chances that the marriage will last because you have already done a lot of the hard work. You have already found out a lot of those difficult facts people who are getting married should know about each other before marriage rather than after, such as how important it is to the husband that his father's stocks stay in his family or the part-ownership the wife has with her family in those apartment buildings in New York.

Not everyone agrees. One woman (who shall remain nameless) was badgered by her parents-in-law-to-be via her husband-to-be to agree to a prenup. She found it insulting. "I wasn't about to marry him until he was ready to make a

One's life does not consist in the abundance of possessions.
LUKE 12:15 NRSV

The amount of money you owe is a symptom, not a problem. The symptom will keep returning if you don't correct the problem.
LARRY BURKETT, MONEY MATTERS

full commitment without hedging his bets!" When he saw how she felt he dropped the matter. (His willingness to stand up to his parents for her meant more than all the financial goodies he ever could have brought into the marriage!)

My heart almost broke with the cruel thought that our marriage is based upon the cold, stern word "duty."

LUCRETIA GARFIELD, IN A LETTER TO HUSBAND PRESIDENT JAMES GARFIELD

"My second wife didn't insist on a prenup," says one now-divorced respondent. "She just substituted an operating principle of 'what's-yours-is-mine-and-what's-mine-is-mine.' She had complete access to my income and assets, but she very carefully kept a separate account for her income. She used it, among other things, to pay the mortgage on her house.

"I didn't realize the significance of this until years later, as it was explained to me by my divorce attorney: So long as the house payments were made with *her* money and not *our* money, I would never have even an indirect interest in the increased equity the house built up while we were married. I didn't really care about that—it was understood from the beginning it was *her* house. What hurt was the implicit distrust and pettiness behind it."

Certainly it makes good sense for any family to have wills. And for couples who come together with other people on either side with a financial interest in the family, it is a necessity.

In fact, john and Lillian say it was Lillian's prenuptial agreement that finally allowed them to decide to marry. Lillian had a lovely home filled with antique furniture, had many investments and had been the beneficiary of a large life insurance policy on her deceased husband. She was comfortable financially.

For John, it was a different story. As missionaries in Guatemala, he and his first wife had been able to save very little. His wife's illness and death had actually left him with a large mortgage on their house in Missouri. Being the generous person she is, Lillian was happy to share her assets with John. But John was insistent that they consult an attorney and make sure that everything would eventually be left to Lillian's children. He is the one who suggested a prenup.

"Lillian would never have asked for it, but I know it was on her mind," John said. "It was better that it came from me. And, really, this is how it should be."

Shortly after marrying in 1998, we—Dan and Kay—set up a family living trust. It's essentially a will, not a prenuptial, but it has the best features of both. It provides for the disposal of our estate under various circumstances, including if one should precede the other in death. In that case, the balance of our retirement and other accounts would go to the surviving spouse.

QUESTION:
How would you describe your current standard of living? Are you satisfied with it? Do you earn enough to continue to meet it?

However, upon the death of both of us, the estate would then go to our children and other named lesser beneficiaries. Although the liquid assets left in the estate would be divided more or less equally among our four children, Kay's house would go to her children alone while other specific items— family heirlooms and things of more sentimental value— would be set aside for individual heirs on both sides. Exactly how and what would go to whom we predetermined largely by the expressed and agreed-to desires of the individual children or other heirs.

Will, trust or prenuptial agreement—however you word it, if you have things you want to stay in your family, make sure it is understood between the two of you and that it is arranged for legally. It doesn't have to take the romance out of your marriage. It isn't planning for a divorce or for your spouse's death. It is securing your family with wisdom and foresight.

Oh, and to all you couples who have two different financial philosophies: this is not necessarily a bad thing. It can have a good side. Our first married-couple respondents pointed this out. "He's a good balance to my conservative nature," she said, "and I'm a good balance to his 'buy-it-all' nature. When I get worried about money, he makes it work."

One last thing. The complete quote from which we took this chapter's title can be found in 1 Timothy 6:10: "For the love of money is a root of all kinds of evil." Note those two words *love of*. There is nothing wrong with money per se. Feel free to be just as prosperous together as you possibly can be. But remember to be good stewards of all that God entrusts to you. And hold your wealth lightly, remembering Jesus' words in Matthew 6:19-21:

> Do not store up for yourselves treasures on earth, where moth and rust destroy, and where thieves break in and steal. But store up for yourselves treasures in heaven, where moth and rust do not destroy, and where thieves do not break in and steal. For where your treasure is, there your heart will be also.

FOR DISCUSSION

On the first graph, rate yourself from one to five in your handling of financial matters. Then on the second graph, rate your spouse from one to five in his or her handling of financial matters. How can you work out a joint financial approach that will best benefit your family?

Money, like ambition, is a good servant, but both are bad masters.

SIR FRANCIS BACON

Honor the LORD with your wealth; . . . then your barns will be filled to overflowing.

PROVERBS 3:9-10

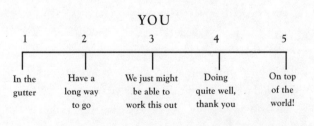

YOU

1	2	3	4	5
In the gutter	Have a long way to go	We just might be able to work this out	Doing quite well, thank you	On top of the world!

YOUR SPOUSE

1	2	3	4	5
Really has problems	Quite a way to go	I think we can work together	Actually quite impressive	Nigh near perfect!

Where Will We Call Home?

If you're a couple over thirty-five, you likely fall into one of two categories: either you're already married and are living *somewhere* with your spouse, or you are approaching the altar and may still be figuring this one out. You who are already married also fall into one of two more groups: those who are perfectly content with your living arrangements, and those who, for whatever reason, may be having second thoughts about them.

Whatever group you're in, your residence options boil down to two:

• Live in one or the other's place.

• Live in a "new" place (at least, new to the two of you).

Before thou marry make sure of a house wherein to tarry.

Each option has both *tangible* and *intangible* aspects to consider.

TANGIBLES VERSUS INTANGIBLES

We are not here to say which is more important: *tangible* considerations like money and expenses, or *intangible* considerations like feelings and adjustments. All we know is, the most logical decisions regarding tangibles ("It's cheaper to live in my house") can be undone eventually if important intangibles ("I don't feel at home here") are not considered and allowed for.

The *key intangible* seems to be just how comfortable, accepted and *welcome* both partners feel, regardless of where they choose to call home and whatever the inequities may be in their degrees of ownership. And that feeling is built on the covenant that the marriage relationship itself is rock-solid and primary, that nothing else—not a house, or money, or cars, or careers, or even the emotional tug-of-war that kids or in-laws sometimes set up—can ever come between you or your commitment to one another.

If a house is divided against itself, that house cannot stand.
MARK 3:25

For those with younger kids, the acceptance of a home by stepchildren is a major consideration as well. Perhaps a spouse can adjust to living in the other's home, but can his or her children make that adjustment as easily? Or will they feel like guests who are not entirely welcome in a home they had no say in choosing and to which they have no emotional attachment?

The *key tangible* seems to be the sizable asset that a home can represent. For many, if not most people, a home is the largest single investment they hold. Depending on circumstances, it is not unusual today for a homeowner to have tens or even hundreds of thousands of dollars of equity in that property. Small wonder, then, that the decision to share that investment with someone else is not so much the issue as is *how* they will share that property—as we've touched on in chapter three.

Now if, after saying all that, one of you can move smoothly into the other's home, so much the better. But if that comfort can come only by finding a new home, then start shopping.

OPTION ONE:
LIVING IN THE OTHER'S HOME

What we discovered—and it surprised us—is that the majority of those we interviewed and surveyed chose option one, though often with some interesting variations that made it something like option two. For example, one couple now married about three years decided to live in her home, but made many changes that have helped make it "theirs."

Bless this house,
O Lord we pray,
Make it safe by
night and day;
Bless these walls, so
firm and stout,
Keeping want and
trouble out.

HELEN TAYLOR,
BLESS THIS HOUSE

"Since I was renting and my wife had just purchased a very large new home, it made it easy to move in without the feeling that I was a visitor in a well-established home," the husband explained. "At first it was just I that moved in after our marriage. Eight months later we were joined by my three young daughters."

Despite the fact the house was both big and new, they customized it even further, especially after his daughters joined them permanently.

She, the owner, said, "We put a pool in, landscaping, made more room for the girls, and we even redid the entire upstairs."

Even though this was an expensive proposition, neither seemed to mind it. In fact, they both seemed to relish the opportunity to build something together that would unite their families and represent a visible, physical commitment to one another.

Some couples, in deciding to make one or the other's house their permanent home, also find ways to make the sharing more equitable. Sophie liked her home and living in the city and was glad that Russell was agreeable to moving in with her after they married.

As for Russell, he was both flexible and creative: "I had always wanted to live in the Bay Area, so we decided to live in Sophie's home, despite the fact that for the first year and a half I had to commute ninety miles to work. I spent two nights a week in a hotel in the town where I worked, and worked Fridays from our home. Sophie owned our house, so I bought out half the equity."

Russell now owns a half-interest in *their* shared home, but not everyone wants to, needs to or is able to put up enough money to do the same. For one thing, most after-thirty-five marriages are second marriages, more frequently the result of divorce than the death of a first spouse. Many divorced people—more often men than women—are already paying to help support a first family. That being the case, maybe you, like they, simply haven't got the wherewithal to make significant payments for a second home and family.

Nor does owning a part of the home seem to be the most determining factor in feeling accepted, welcome and comfortable. Many couples we've talked with have managed to create a sense of "our" home from what is, essentially, a sole-owner situation. Who actually owns the home just doesn't seem to be an issue.

One older man did not purchase any of his new wife's equity, but he nonetheless found he was very happy and relaxed living in her house. He says, "This was easy. I was renting—she owned a home that was blocks from my work. She is a great homemaker and wanted me to live in her home. She was living by herself. Plus, this was not the home of her previous marriage."

We can't say for sure whether age is a factor in this or not, though the older couples seemed to have the least trouble simply moving into the other's home. Lillian and John are in their seventies and eighties, and John had no real trouble adjusting to living in Lillian's house.

Another couple we surveyed are in their early seventies and late sixties. He, unlike John, was *initially* nervous about

May the LORD make the woman who is coming into your home like Rachel and Leah, who together built up the house of Israel.

RUTH 4:11

moving into her home but got past that quickly. "I was concerned as to whether she would want to have me live in her home. Actually, it was a no-brainer. As I pointed out to her, as an alternative I could offer her a 10-by-14-foot room with me at my daughter's house, with bathroom privileges, providing she could move faster than my two grandsons."

Our last instance is a couple, relative newlyweds, in their late sixties and fifties. Speaking for the youngest of our three examples, the wife explains that "He had already decided before the engagement that he didn't want to move from Colorado. However, after visiting Arizona several times—I lived there—he would have seriously considered moving there, but I told him that I would be willing to move instead. We are happily living in Colorado now, but think we would also have been happy living in my home in Arizona."

The way they resolved the "who-moves" issue was for her to move into his home, where she is now very comfortable and settled. That feeling of comfort and security is the product of both his efforts to make her welcome and at ease, and of her use of little touches to make it her home, without intruding on his sense of domain.

Other ideas we've heard for transforming a home that just one of you owns into a home both can feel is "ours" are these:

1. Take all the combined furniture from both partners and put it out on the lawn or driveway. Then from among all the stuff pick and choose the pieces you both like best. Put only that back, and then store, sell or give away the rest.

2. Take everything off the walls and redo all the pictures and other hangings.

3. Replace most or all the furnishings, including carpet

By wisdom a house is built, and through understanding it is established.

PROVERBS 24:3

and drapes, by buying all new stuff together. Many older couples find they are long overdue for this anyway.

4. Repaint or put up new wallpaper as part of redecorating.

Neither John nor the other older gentleman were homeowners at the time they married their present wives. The woman from Arizona, on the other hand, did have her own home, which she sold. That's not uncommon. At least some of the proceeds of the equity from that home could then be invested in the home of her new spouse. This arrangement not only provides a new spouse with a sense of ownership, it also makes sure that if the equity in the spouse's home continues to grow, both partners will share in it. That's essentially what Russell did.

Another option, however, is to keep the empty home and convert it to rental property. How the title is held, who has what interest in which home, how the liabilities are shared, how the income will be used—these are matters to discuss before you marry. (Or, if you are already married, to discuss *now!*)

Although most of the couples in our survey tell us they are quite comfortably settled into one or the other's home, it sometimes took quite a while to achieve that state of acceptance. Sadly, sometimes that acceptance never comes— the marriage ends instead, and that's exactly what we want to help prevent.

Peace be to this house.

LUKE 10:5

Paula and Clifford have been sharing her home for eighteen years now. Still, despite all their best efforts, it wasn't easy at first.

"Many people advised us to find a new home, not stay in the same house because of memories and ghosts of the past," Paula said. "We looked for many months and found nothing we liked better than my paid-for home in the hills overlooking the city. The thought of house payments at our age was most unappealing. I adjusted better than I anticipated to sharing my home with a second husband. We did have some problems with my nineteen-year-old son, who had assumed the head of the household since his father moved out, and Clifford was the intruder in his domain. Time and my son's departure for college eased the transition."

Compared to Paula and Clifford, our transition to one home was relatively easy, at least in terms of "ghosts of the past." Still, it was not without its own form of pain and loss.

In 1990 a huge fire had swept Santa Barbara, destroying over six hundred homes, including ninety-five in Kay's neighborhood. Miraculously, only one person was killed as the fire raged for a day and a night. Kay's family's home and everything in it was one of the casualties. It took awhile to deal with the loss and all the necessary adjustments, but she set about rebuilding before the year was out. The new home was markedly different from the original, with everything in it brand-new and changed—no ghosts.

Back in 1984 Dan had sold his home and given away or sold most of the original furnishings from his first marriage. His wife had died of cancer, and he subsequently made a series of decisions he now sees as hasty and foolish. But he didn't see it that way then, and one ultimate good result when marrying Kay was—no issue over where to live or whose furnishings to keep. Again, no ghosts.

Happy homes are built with blocks of patience.

In addition, all four of our children were adults and out on their own by that time, so there were none of the potential problems that sometimes accompany dealing with one another's kids. Not that that was ever of real concern—all our offspring and their spouses get along remarkably well with one another as well as with us.

Another spin on the problem of where to live when they

decided to marry was shared by Nancy and Jeff. They met while both were traveling on business—attending different conventions at the same large hotel. They soon found that courtship is a lot harder when you live a thousand miles apart, yet they managed it for quite some time. When they finally decided to marry, weather, rather than geography, was the deciding factor as to where they would live.

"It was an easy decision," Nancy said. "Jeff hated the cold, and I was from North Dakota. He was living in Florida and loving it, so he asked me to move there. I readily agreed. He loves Tampa, and I came to love it too. But at first it was a little too close to his 'ex,' who lived only two miles from us (and still does). I have come to accept this, and now it doesn't bother me."

Another of our respondents tells us that when he met and later married his wife in northern California, the decision of where to live was also somewhat forced by circumstances. All the same, he has no regrets. He tells us, "There wasn't much deciding; it was her place. At the time I was a year into a new business and had put all my worth into it. I was living at the shop so a 'home' I did not have."

The situation is different still for Maureen and James, who share his home in Dallas. "I had just bought a house with a friend six months before James and I were engaged," Maureen says. "He had bought a house with his sister. We decided to live in his house because it was larger. However, I still don't think of it as my house, and we've been married almost ten years." She adds that Dallas housing prices make it difficult to buy a different one now.

It's sad to hear that one of the marriage partners still does not feel "at home," even after ten years. It's also difficult to say exactly what they need to do to correct that situation, but our experience tells us they really need to.

Ways to Make a House Our Home:

* _____
* _____
* _____
* _____
* _____
* _____

Another after-thirty-five, second-marriage-for-both couple from San Diego saw their once-promising relationship end in divorce after just a few years. His never really feeling "at home" was certainly a factor in their breakup.

Although they both owned substantial homes—his was newer but smaller with four bedrooms—she insisted she could not live in his place. "The kitchen's too small," she said. "And anyway there isn't enough room to put up family for holidays and special occasions."

She had a point—her six-bedroom home was better suited for entertaining and accommodating her brood of seven. (Only two were still at home but the others popped in frequently.) Plus, she often had a large number of stay-over guests. She was also quick to point out that her neighborhood was more prestigious than his location.

Overall, however, it wasn't the house, or its location, or its size that caused all the dissention. He recalls, "Even though I sold my home and moved myself and my two kids into her house, I could tell right away that we were a low priority in her life. She simply valued other things more than she did me or mine. For one thing, she had no intention of letting me invest in her equity—she wanted her home in her name only. For another, she had two informal sets of rules—one for us, another for hers. Ours were rigid and rather harsh, hers were much more lax and spottily applied. Basically, it boiled down to an attitude, sometimes explicitly expressed, of 'This is my house, and if you don't like the way I do things, you can leave any time.' So after three frustrating years, I did."

For this couple, the marriage commitment was *not* "rock-solid and primary." Other issues were a higher priority. It was not so much the home and where they chose to live that mattered, it was the attitude behind it. The house was sim-

To forgive the incessant provocations of daily life . . . how can we do it? Only, I think, by remembering where we stand, by meaning our words when we say our prayers each night: "Forgive us our trespasses as we forgive those who trespass against us."

C. S. LEWIS,
THE WEIGHT OF GLORY

ply the embodiment of bigger issues they were reluctant or unable to resolve. Regardless of the apparent issue, whenever there is an attitude of inequality, of one partner having the upper hand for whatever reason, severe problems will almost certainly follow.

OPTION TWO: THE "NEW" PLACE

Indeed, the tangible and practical issue of cost often rules out the option of a new home both can share right from the beginning. Yet as a version of that, the second-most-popular option seemed to be starting out in one or the other's home, then sooner or later moving into a different place—for lots of different reasons.

Andrea says, "Scott owned a home when we started dating, and so after we married I moved into his house. However, he had bought the house from his grandfather's estate—more for his family's convenience that his own needs (it was still full of his grandparents' and deceased sister's stuff, and there was barely room in the nine hundred square feet for his things, let alone mine). In retrospect, I wish we had found a new place of our own right away. Happily, we just finished building our first home together and settled in just a little past our second anniversary. It's a beautiful home, and I can see us settling here for life, something I've never been able to say about any other place I've lived before."

Scott adds, "Although that first house was small, it was easier in many respects to just move in there. After a while though, we realized it just wasn't big enough for two or more persons to live in comfortably, so we decided to build a place of our own. Building a home together was sometimes a frustrating process; I can see where it could do lasting damage to a relationship, but in our case we weathered the storm quite well, I believe."

Home, they say, is where the heart is. What makes your heart feel at home?

- _____
- _____
- _____
- _____
- _____
- _____

Mark and Rebecca also had problems trying to share a small home, especially with Rebecca's young daughter living with them. But the house's small size wasn't the only problem, as Mark explains: "Rebecca owned a house and I was living in an apartment. It was a natural for me to move into her place. But this house was very small, plus Rebecca's ex-husband had a strong tendency to think of it as 'his' house and tried to create trouble over it. So within the first year of our marriage we sold the house and moved across town to a bigger home."

Therefore everyone who hears these words of mine and puts them into practice is like a wise man who built his house on the rock. . . . It did not fall, because it had its foundation on the rock

MATTHEW 7:24-25

Financially difficult, no question—but they felt other, intangible considerations were more important, so they did it anyway.

Another couple, older than Mark and Rebecca and with no children still at home, made a decision very similar to the younger couple's. He says, "This was easy. The lease on her apartment was up the month we were to be married and I owned a home. We agreed to find a home new to both of us as quickly as possible and we did, although it took longer than had been expected."

John and Lillian relocated to a "start-over" home for both of them, eventually. Married in their early seventies and now approaching their eighties, they had yet another set of considerations. This is how Lillian explains it: "We both wanted to retire in a more temperate climate, so after checking out options in both Florida and Arizona, we mutually agreed on Arizona.

"Since this was a second marriage, we both felt that the best gift we could give our children would be to enter a continuing care retirement facility. This would relieve the children from the burden of caring for their elderly parents—especially in the case of stepparents. As a result, we chose to move to a retirement community outside Phoenix in 1997."

Sometimes, when geography is a factor, it isn't quite so easy to decide who will move where. Take Anthony and Lynn's situation, for instance. Anthony recalls, "At the time I accepted my job, Lynn and I had talked about marriage, but had not made a definite commitment to one another. Lynn was teaching at the seminary where she had attended, in Louisville, on her second one-year contract, but was not clear what her long-term professional plans would be. So there was little question of my joining Lynn in Kentucky—the only feasible option at the time was for her to join me in Maine."

For Peter and Janet, the new-home decision wasn't quite so cut-and-dried. Janet recalls that "even though I had a teaching job and a lovely condo in Hawaii, I was open to moving. After a visit to New England I liked it a lot and agreed to be the one to move. We decided that I would move partly because Peter was making a bit more money than I and also because I was ready to stop working for a while. After marriage, I moved into his apartment, leaving my condo full of belongings and furniture for a time.

"Peter was very accommodating when I moved in, clearing out closets and drawers for my clothes and accepting my indoor cat. He even let me move furniture around and make the apartment more cozy and attractive even before my furniture arrived from Hawaii. He was also patient about giving me directions to get around and to find places I wanted to go. It was a very fun time for me since I really love finding out about new places and people."

Peter explains that the time in his apartment was relatively temporary, and before long they were moving into a home of their own. "Janet sold her condo and volunteered to follow me back to Massachusetts so there was no argument and no debate. We moved into my apartment and within four months had moved into a 'fixer-upper' that occupied us for

A house of dreams untold, It looks out over the treetops, And faces the setting sun.

EDWARD MACDOWELL, FROM A LOG CABIN

I discovered I always have choices and sometimes it's only a choice of attitude.

JUDITH M. KNOWLTON

the next eight years. We went on from there to a house in Cambridge and into our present residence in Boston."

Janet and Peter eventually adopted two children, so their home decisions were also affected by the need for more room for their growing family. But with or without children, many people long for a "dream home" of their own.

The eagle nestles
near the sun;
The dove's
low nest for me!
The eagle's on the
crag; sweet one,
The dove's in our
green tree!

JOHN JAMES PIATT,
A SONG OF CONTENT

"When we first married we moved into my condo, where I'd lived for twelve years," explained a middle-aged woman who had been married four years. "I owned it, and that was a very good feeling. Security is important to me, as is the need to 'nest' that many women feel. I am an educated woman and have worked for many years, but my home is very important to me. I had dreamed for many, many years of leaving the large, congested city where we lived as I grew up and where I returned after college.

"After a few years I longed to buy a house, one away from where we were living, away from where I'd spent most of my life. However, I think I underestimated the process, how stressful it would be and also how expensive. I also did not truly understand my husband's position about money and how it may be used. We did wind up making a large investment of his savings into a home with the understanding that this allocation would always be his to have back if he so chose.

"So, we moved into my dream house three years after we were married and I simply love it. I love being able to nest, but would also love to entertain much more."

Listen to his take on the same story: "When we first married, I moved from my apartment into my wife's condo because it was larger. It was a little small for both of us, and we wanted to get out of the area where she lived, so we talked about desirable characteristics of the 'ideal town' where we might move and what each of us wanted, then narrowed down the choices.

"I felt like she narrowed down the choices too much, leaving only one city that she would accept. I didn't state strongly enough that I wanted to explore more options and didn't particularly like the one that she had chosen, mostly because it involved spending a lot more money on housing than I thought was reasonable for us. It's working out and I'm becoming adjusted to our new home, but the process of getting here was unpleasant for me."

Again, we cannot tell you just what will make or break your decision of where you should live. But as we saw in the example of the couple from San Diego, made the wrong way or for the wrong reasons, such a decision can make or break a marriage. Did he or she ever really make a true commitment to the other in the first place? Or did one or both of them let the material, tangible aspects of money and property get in the way of the intangibles of love and consideration for one another? Did they lose sight of God's intentions for all married people?

Obviously, that couple, like all the other couples whose marriages ended in divorce, had problems they felt they could not resolve. Sooner or later, you and your spouse will face your share of seemingly insurmountable problems as a result of some of your decisions. And maybe they are insurmountable—if left in human hands alone. We believe the good Lord allows adversity in our lives so that we will see our own shortcomings and be driven to him. Rather than retreat, use these times of marital adversity to grow in your love for God and in your strength and commitment to each other.

In the end, the best wisdom of all comes from God's Word:

Unless the LORD builds the house, its builders labor in vain.

Unless the LORD watches over the city, the watchmen stand guard in vain. (Psalm 127:1)

Bless the folk who dwell within; Keep them pure and free from sin; Bless us all that we may be, Fit, O Lord, to dwell with Thee.

HELEN TAYLOR, *BLESS THIS HOUSE*

FOR DISCUSSION

1. Do you both own homes? What will be the basis for deciding whose home you will live in?

   - *Geography*? (Closeness to work, school, friends, grandparents, in-laws and such.)

   - *Size of home*? (Especially relevant if there will be a number of children living with you, more so than in your current home.)

   - *Cost of home*? (Mortgage payments, length of mortgage, taxes, upkeep, amount of equity, overall condition of home, and so forth.)

   - *Attachment to the home*? (Inherited family home, raised children there, custom-built home, other factors.)

2. Does only one of you own a home? Have you thoroughly discussed the options of

   - sharing the existing home of one partner "as is"?

   - buying or renting a "new" home together? If willing, the owning spouse *could*

     rent out the owned home for income to offset the new home rental expense.

     sell the owned property and reinvest the equity in the new home, with or without matching/non-matching investment by the spouse without property.

     refinance the owned home, using the extra money as down payment on a "new home" and still renting out the old home.

   In all cases involving property transfers or changes in title or on deeds, consult both a qualified real estate attorney and an accountant experienced in tax and real estate laws.

5

Yours, Mine and Ours

We came across a tongue-in-cheek "ad" posted on the Internet titled FREE TO A GOOD HOME. On one side is the picture of an adorable little kitten. Underneath is this description: *Beautiful six-mo. old male orange & caramel tabby. Playful, friendly, very affectionate. Ideal for family w/ kids.* On the other side is the picture of a young man in a sweatshirt and a baseball cap. Underneath is this description: *Handsome 32-yr. old husband—personable, funny, good job, but doesn't like cats. Says he goes or cat goes.* Across the bottom of the poster is printed: *Call Jennifer—555-2643—come see both & decide which you'd like.*

The blending of two already established households almost always means that something's got to give somewhere. In our case, we ended up with three cars for two drivers—way more than we needed or felt we could afford. One car belonged to Kay's student son, Eric. That was the easiest car problem to solve—we simply shoved it aside for him with an ultimatum that just as soon as he was out of school he had to come and claim it. (Even that wasn't without some conflict, however. To this day it takes a big chunk of the garage to store.) The second was a nice, sensible sedan—Dan's car. The third was a spiffy, impractical sporty model—Kay's car.

Both of us were exceedingly attached to our own car, and neither cared all that much for the other one's car. After much soul searching, a great deal of discussion and a few tears on the part of at least one of us, we decided to sell both our cars and get one vehicle we both liked—one that didn't have that *yours* or *mine* emotional tag attached.

So what *does* a couple do about the extra furniture that won't fit into the new apartment? What about the sweet cat the other person is allergic to? How about the beloved orange and yellow picture Aunt Louise painted that is, to put it delicately, not exactly the new spouse's idea of living room quality? What about his chili-pepper-shaped Christmas lights that look simply awful with her matching crystal ornaments?

EMOTIONAL ATTACHMENT

Just for the sake of argument, let's start the discussion with the sometimes murderously volatile pet issue. Say husband has a dog and wife can't stand dogs. She hates that dog hair all over everything. She's totally fed up with the barking, even if it is, as husband says, just the dog's way of "protecting" her. Wife simply cannot abide the way that canine has taken over the house. That smelly dog has really come between the two of them, and she has let husband know her feelings in the matter. But he says he loves the dog and he won't give it up.

Hopeless situation, right?

Not so fast. It's clear that husband has an emotional attachment to his pooch, and if he were forced to give the dog up, he would resent it long after the dog hair was vacuumed up and the last of the dog chow gone and forgotten. On the other hand, it's also clear that wife is no dog lover. The goal here is to take this emotional problem and balance it out with quality and with quantity. Look at what we mean:

QUESTION:
Are there things
that have been
causing either
of you anxiety?
What are they?

- _____
- _____
- _____
- _____
- _____
- _____

First, *quality*. To affect the quality of the pet, husband could

- Have the dog spayed or neutered. This just might quiet the pooch down and possibly make him easier for wife to abide.

- Get obedience training. A well-behaved dog is so much more enjoyable to be around. And if both partners attend the training with the dog, it just might help wife bond with the pooch too.

- Clean and vacuum frequently so that there won't be such a problem with dog hair. Also, husband could invest in lint rollers so that dog hair could easily be removed from clothing and furniture. (No, it isn't a good idea to ask wife to do this cleaning!) And while he's at it, he could teach the dog not to get up on the furniture in the first place—although that may go back to the point about obedience training.

Second, *quantity*. To affect the quantity of time wife has to spend with the dog, husband might:

- Make sure wife has a sanctuary where the dog is not allowed.

- Give the dog an area all its own, too—at least a bed. But preferably also a place to exercise.

Perhaps you don't have a pet problem. Perhaps your troubles are much greater than that. Hang on. We're just getting started.

Janet's emotional attachment was to her family, her friends and everything she had ever known. That's a lot to be asked to leave when you marry at thirty-six. "After our wedding in Honolulu, I prepared for our departure to Boston," she

The quality of mercy is not strained. . . . It blesseth him that gives and him that takes.

SHAKESPEARE,
THE MERCHANT OF
VENICE

recalls. "I was leaving everything and I sobbed hysterically. But Peter and I prayed together, and I truly did receive confirmation from God that everything was under his control, and I never cried again. That's not to say that things were easy. I had barely met Peter's large family, and their arguing, yelling and manipulating were really tough for me to handle. But Peter let me know from the start that he was on my side. He loved his family, but our marriage was his first priority. He also let his parents and his sisters know this, by the way."

Love is the balm that eases the friction between two people who have committed their lives to each other. Apply the healing balm often.

For Clifford, the emotional attachment he had to release was the small church he had attended for years. He knew everyone there and everyone knew him. Paula's church was a totally different story. With over a thousand members, it had a great deal to offer, but it seemed so impersonal. Still, Paula was active in the choir—an interest Clifford shared—and in a close-knit Sunday school class as well as in a variety of other ministries. Clifford knew it made far more sense for them to attend Paula's church than his, but still it was difficult.

Let's see how the principles of *quality* and *quantity* can be applied to Janet's and Clifford's situations:

Janet's move from Honolulu to Boston:

Quality: What the quality of the move would do to enhance Janet's life.

- Janet is a teacher. A big part of the reason for their move is the very high wages in the suburb where they will be settling. Should Janet choose to work—either full or part time—she will make substantially more than she was earning.

- She can consider working on the advanced degree she has talked about so long.

- She can map out the advantages of living in a large, historic city, with its many cultural areas nearby—something that is very appealing to Janet.

Quantity: How she might use her time to help herself adjust.

- Because of the added income, Janet can plan on several visits "home" each year.

- Janet's need for a quieter, slower pace might be met by the couple purchasing or renting a weekend cottage for the two of them—no extended family included, by the way.

Clifford's move from his small church to Paula's large church:

Quality: What the change would do to enhance Clifford's spiritual life.

- Together, Clifford and Paula can look over the varied ministries the larger church has to offer and decide together where they want to be involved. It won't necessarily be in Paula's old tracks.

- They can visit various Sunday school classes and, again, decide together which one they prefer. At his old church, there was only one adult class.

Quantity: How he might adjust his time to help with the transition.

- Clifford doesn't have to cut ties with his friends at the old church. He and Paula can plan to have them over periodically.

- They can visit the little church now and then—attend special events such as the Christmas program or visit on a Sunday now and then.

It doesn't happen all at once.
You become.
It takes a long time.

MARGERY WILLIAMS,
THE VELVETEEN RABBIT

QUESTION:
How can you apply the principles of quality and quantity to your situation?

Stuff and Stuff and More Stuff

Let's face it: when you have two houses full of stuff, and you're moving all of it into one place, there's bound to be a problem. We heard about it again and again on the surveys couples filled out. One lady, from Washington, tactfully commented that since her house was already full it was a little hard to decide where to put her new husband's stuff when he moved in. And, she admitted, after four years of marriage "a lot of his things are still in boxes." (See again our suggestions in chapter four on ideas for "blending" two sets of possessions.)

Clifford didn't see two houses full of stuff as such a big problem. He figured, "Paula is a great decorator so I was happy to let her decide what stayed and what went." (Not the same story we got from Paula, by the way. "I think it was hard to combine possessions," she told us. "I do love to decorate, and I have very strong ideas on how it should be done. At the same time, I didn't want to hurt Clifford's feelings if I didn't agree with his tastes." A comment like that raises a whole separate set of issues, doesn't it?)

Many people told us they were relatively unattached to most of their "things." Russell willingly sold the majority of his household items—with the exception of a handmade walnut roll-top desk and his stereo system. "Our home is furnished largely as it was when Sophie was single," he says.

Think back to that parenthetical comment of Paula's. Most couples who answered our survey didn't make a big deal about the things they had to toss in order to fit into one home. And yet . . .

Whose stuff *is* the best? And who *does* make the final decision on what stays and what goes?

"I had to put my stereo in the basement because the speakers were too big, according to Sophie," said Russell. "I

You know, by the time you reach my age, you've made plenty of mistakes, and if you have lived your life properly, so you learn.
You put things in perspective.
You pull your energies together.
You change.
You go forward.

Ronald Reagan

love to listen to music, and Sophie's stereo wasn't as good as mine, so I had to give this up for a while. But once she finally heard my stereo she relented. She could hear the superior sound. We even purchased an entertainment center which she says balances the size of the speakers."

"I think it's a mistake to let just one person make all the important decisions about what stays and what goes," Dan adds. "My second wife just about insisted I get rid of all my stuff when I sold my house and moved into hers with my kids. So while my house was in escrow we had a giant 'every-thing-must-go' sale in my driveway, and by the end of the first day nearly everything from my previous life was gone—books, pictures, knick-knacks and mementos, as well as furniture and larger pieces. That night I was physically ill, which I attributed at the time to too much sun. Later I realized I was just reacting to too big a loss, too soon, and all at once."

A ROSE BY ANY OTHER NAME . . .

"Letting go of so much that I worked hard for for so long was difficult," said one female respondent, married for the first time at age forty. "I'd been single and on my own since I left home at nineteen. When I married my husband I gave up my house and my furniture, but I kept my maiden name. Shortly before my third baby was born, I gave up my maiden name too. I finally turned my focus on what I had gained by my marriage rather than on what I had left behind."

Interestingly, that name change has been a stickler for us, too, although for a different reason.

Kay says, "I had a wonderful maiden name. It was Marshall. No one ever mispronounced it; no one ever misspelled it. When I was in school, teachers always did everything alpha-betically, so I never had to give a report first, and I never had to wait until last. I always got the coveted right-in-the-middle

There is a time for everything, and a season for every activity under heaven.

ECCLESIASTES 3:1

spot. Yet when I married my first husband, Larry, I never thought twice about changing my name to Strom. Even though Kay Strom sounded like two rocks dropping, taking her husband's name was just something a wife did back then.

"When I married Dan, however, things were different. First, I had an established writing name. I had over twenty books out under the name of Kay Marshall Strom, and if I changed my name to Kline, I would lose the name recognition I had worked hard to achieve. Second, Kay Kline just didn't sound that good to my ear. I didn't want to change my name again. Besides, things had changed in the twenty-plus years since my first marriage. Now it was not that uncommon for women to keep their names after marriage. So despite various and sundry advice against it . . . and the confusion it caused . . . and in a few cases, downright disapproval, I kept my name Kay Marshall Strom."

Yes, we still have some confused people and a few lifted eyebrows. An occasional letter comes addressed to Mr. and Mrs. Dan Marshall Strom. But for the most part our decision to stick with *yours* and *mine* names has worked just fine.

When we check into a hotel we switch into our *ours* name, and we are Mr. and Mrs. Dan Kline. We like switching *yours* and *mine* over to *ours*.

Ours

The blending of *yours* and *mine* into *ours* goes far beyond material things. It goes beyond emotional mindset. It goes all the way to the heart.

"I had been single for over six years," Paula reflected. "I was used to sleeping alone. When I first married Clifford, I kept waking up all night every time he turned over. I finally got used to someone else being in bed with me again. Now it's hard to sleep by myself."

If two lie down together, they will keep warm. But how can one keep warm alone?

Ecclesiastes 4:11

Listen to Sophie, a woman so independent it would annoy her whenever she came in the front door and Russell would call down from upstairs, "Sophie?"

"I would ask myself, *Well who else would it be?!* Now if I come home and Russell's not there to call down 'Sophie?' I really miss it. There is just something so special about the comforting assurance of his voice."

As we write this, former President and Mrs. Ronald Reagan are celebrating their fiftieth wedding anniversary. That's an amazing achievement for a couple married after the age of thirty-five—well, at least *he* was over thirty-five.

How did the Reagans make it so long, through so much?

"I've been asked over and over again if there is a secret to staying married for this long and I'd have to say there isn't one," Nancy Reagan said when interviewed by Jeff Wilson of the Associated Press. "Marriage is never fifty-fifty. One of you is always giving more, always compromising. And we've both done our share of compromising in these fifty years."[1]

Compromising. That's it, you know. Throwing the *yours* and the *mine* in together and coming up with more and more *ours*. And then clinging to it tenaciously.

Relationships require compromise, not ultimatums. If you truly love each other, you will try to work it out.

ROBIN FROM CALIFORNIA

FOR DISCUSSION

Does one of you have a pet about which the other is less than excited?

☐ Yes   ☐ No

Will (did) one of you have to give up your church to attend the other's church?

☐ Yes   ☐ No

[1]Jeff Wilson, "Inseparable Reagans Mark a Poignant 50th," *Santa Barbara News Press*, March 4, 2002, p. A3.

Is one of you going to (or did you) get rid of the majority of your possessions?

☐ Yes   ☐ No

Has one of you had to move away from your family and friends?

☐ Yes   ☐ No

Does one of you consider the other's Christmas decorations not of good enough quality to be displayed?

☐ Yes   ☐ No

Does one of you feel you have done most of the giving up of "mine" for the sake of "ours"?

☐ Yes   ☐ No

Every "yes" answer means you as a couple need to talk about potential conflicts and resentments. This is especially true if one of you answered "yes" to the last question. If this is difficult or resentment seems high, it would be wise to have a counselor help you sort through your options.

A Flexible Backbone

W̶hat counts in making a happy marriage is not so much how compatible you are, but how you deal with incompatibility." So wrote Leo Tolstoy over a hundred and fifty years ago. What did he know about it, you ask? Well, for starters, he would have come mighty close to qualifying for this book. He was just months short of thirty-five when he married Sonya Andreyevna. And what with all the death and revolution and social injustice he endured before that, he certainly had his share of baggage to carry into his marriage.

Were Leo Tolstoy to see us, he just might sneer and insist that we know absolutely nothing about what it means to be flexible. But he would be wrong. Last Christmas, for instance, we two were joined by five family members for the afternoon and evening: Dan's son, Kay's daughter and son-in-law who were preparing to file for divorce, Dan's mother-in-law from his first marriage and Kay's father-in-law from her first marriage. It turned out to be a lovely day. But it was also a day that required flexibility with a capital F.

There are two ways of meeting difficulties. You alter the difficulties or you alter yourself to meet them.

PHYLLIS BOTTOME,
NOVELIST

SCENARIOS THAT BEND YOU OUT OF SHAPE

Our Christmas was nothing compared to the flexibility-challenging scenarios other couples told us about.

"I have proof that Paula is an angel," Clifford told us. "We were married for just nine months when my eighty-eight-year-old mother, who could no longer live alone, moved in with us. We had her in our home for about a year and a half as she became increasingly feeble. She finally went into the hospital and then had to be moved to a nursing home. What a strain to put on a brand-new marriage! But Paula couldn't have been nicer."

And then there's the couple with a blended family of five kids, all of them young and at home. At the time they married, the husband was in an apartment by himself and saw his three daughters only once a month, at best. Then when he moved into his wife's house with her two teenage sons, his three little girls began to visit every other weekend. Six months after the wedding the little girls moved in full time. Huge adjustment!

Here's one more: When one middle-aged couple, now in their fourth year of marriage, joined their lives together, they found they needed a whole lot of compromise and a good deal of looking the other way. "We have been through so many transitions since our marriage," the wife told us. "I lost my mother, we moved from a big city to a small town where we knew no one, I was laid off from two jobs, and most important, my husband had huge health challenges."

Two years earlier they had moved from their state's busiest city. Within weeks he was hospitalized with real but varied complaints. After a week in the hospital—with no insurance because of her new job—he was diagnosed with Chronic Fatigue Syndrome, an insidious illness that has kept him debilitated for the past two years, with no end in sight. All that with no support in the new town, a job that didn't

And we know that in all things God works for the good of those who love him, who have been called according to his purpose.

ROMANS 8:28

work out, big debts from the hospital—talk about challenges that require adjustments!

Flexibility is the key word in any marriage. But when people marry at an older age, they have more life experiences to factor into their "unexpected" equation. Granted, a major health disability in mid-life means real changes, but then so does any family health problem. Moving three more little ones into the house—or an eighty-eight-year-old mama—shortly after the honeymoon is a big adjustment, but so is making accommodations for any unexpected family member. So are ill parents (children, parents-in-law, ex-parents-in-law, grandchildren, etc.). So are unexpected debts. So is having to incorporate a different approach to money and the way it is spent. So are unplanned-for roles ("men's work" versus "women's work," "that's your job" versus "keep your hands off, I'll do that the *right* way"). So are those individual quirks you can't believe you didn't see when you were dating, or the ones that only become irritating after you married.

James was refreshingly candid as he reflected on his entrance into married life: "I was settled in my ways and in how I liked to do things and have things done. I gave up some of my personal security when I married and then became a father—three times over! I wasn't used to taking so much responsibility for other people, or sharing my life with someone else." It does require change, and change can be hard.

HOW FLEXIBLE ARE YOU?

So which best describes you? (Okay, after you find *you*, go ahead and see which describes your spouse.)

- *Mighty oak:* staunchly immovable.

- *Holly bush:* lovely to look at, but don't dare try to make adjustments.

A couple can pull a heavier load together than each can pull alone. That's what commitment is all about.

QUESTION:
How has being married to your spouse made you a better person?

Life is change.
Growth is optional.
Choose wisely.

KAREN KAISER-CLARK,
STATE LEGISLATOR

QUESTION:
What unsettling
changes are you
currently facing?
How can you look
forward to new
areas of growth
through them?

• *Tumbleweed*: blown away by the first hard storm.

• *Sturdy willow*: bends in the wind to where it can withstand almost anything.

There is a lot to be said for an immovable oak—until you find out your daughter is going to have to move back in with you, the daughter who married that young punk you warned her about but she wouldn't listen and you said "Don't come crying to me when he breaks your heart!" and now she has two kids and a Saint Bernard, the punk is long gone and she has nowhere else to go.

A holly bush is beautiful—until those cute little girls move in with you for good, including the one who isn't even potty trained yet.

A tumbleweed is refreshingly unique—so long as the honeymoon lasts and the problems don't get too big and the grass isn't greener on the other side of the fence.

The fact is, married life is far easier if at least one of you is a willow. And it is so much more so if you both have at least some willow characteristics.

You say you are not a willow? Or your spouse isn't?

Mark and Rebecca both describe themselves as oaks. "We are so set in our ways," Rebecca says. "We're both very controlling. We spend our money differently, we do our finances differently, we raise our kids differently, we discipline differently. Our biggest battle is learning to be flexible."

Good news, Mark and Rebecca—and all the rest of us. Unlike a tree that is what it is and can never be anything else, *we can change*.

Dan has had to change and adapt many times during the last thirty years: "I've changed careers four times since I was twenty-five, and not one of those changes was planned or foreseen. I'm not complaining, and I wouldn't undo them even if I could. But each was not my choice; they were all forced by events beyond my control.

I've been married three times, when I never intended to marry more than once. I have now settled—quite happily with Kay this time, I might add—into what I hope is my last major adjustment. (Though I suspect God has still more plans for us together.)

I don't think I could ever have held up under all the stress and loss and pain if not for the Lord. I know his hand was in every single step along the way, though he also allowed me to choose each one through that miraculous thing called 'free will.' He led me right to himself and gave me the grace I need to adapt to all the change and to accept all of it as part of his great plan, which, incredibly, includes me."

INCREASING YOUR BENDABILITY QUOTIENT

Yes, however stiff you might be now, you can increase your BQ (bendability quotient). And you'll have plenty of opportunity to perfect your new skill. Life will throw you plenty of opportunities to practice!

An excellent tactic for increasing your BQ is to pre-think some of the possible scenarios that might hit you. For instance, if you or your spouse has elderly parents, the chances are that one of you will at some point have to deal with ill in-laws who need caregivers. What will you do? What part are you prepared to play in their care? Will they live with you? Can you help financially?

This tactic is especially important for people where one partner has children, but is not the custodial parent. Suppose that situation should change. What would happen then? We know of a couple where the new wife told her husband straight out that should he somehow get custody

"For I know the plans I have for you," declares the LORD, "plans to prosper you and not to harm you, plans to give you hope and a future."
JEREMIAH 29:11

QUESTION:
Is there a possible status quo-buster perched on your horizon? What are some possible scenarios for handling it?

of his children, she would leave him. His ex-wife died unexpectedly, his daughters came to live with him, and his wife, true to her word, packed her bags and her own two children and left.

Of course, not all scenarios can be predicted. Certainly the middle-aged couple married four years never imagined his illness, nor the disability and financial problems that resulted. Those are the kinds of things that sneak up and clobber you with no warning.

Make a decision that you and your spouse will train yourselves to see the workings of the Lord every day. What have you seen today?

When changes do come, it's important to stay calm. It's all too easy to respond to unexpected situations with

- anger ("You told your daughter she could do *what?!* Not in my house she won't!")

- ultimatums ("If those kids move in, I move out!")

- threats ("If you spend so much as a dime on that, I'm taking every bit of my money out of our bank account!")

- a battle of wills ("I won't hear of taking care of your parents. If you won't listen to reason about a nursing home, we have nothing to talk about.")

- despair ("That's it! Our marriage is over! We never bargained for anything like this, and, let's face it, it's just more than we can handle.")

Peter, who was single until he was forty, had a number of unexpected changes in his life when he married. "I loved my lazy, lay-around time," he said. "As an elementary school teacher I would sometimes be home by four o'clock, and I would just flop on the couch until well into the evening. And I had a lot of lazy weekend time too. I didn't realize how much I treasured that."

When Peter married Janet, she had other ideas for his free time. Worthwhile ideas—like fixing up the house, and helping in the kitchen, and putting his clothes away, and other things that were not nearly as much fun as lying around. The more Janet nagged, the more Peter balked.

"We finally put our heads together and worked out a perfect solution," Peter reports. "We call it a freedom day. Each month Janet and I each get a day where we can do anything we want. I usually spend mine on the couch with my feet up. I enjoy it more than ever because I look forward to it all month."

A woman in Washington who could not pry her husband away from the computer in the evenings came up with a solution that suited them both. They put the computer in the bedroom. Now, while her husband pecks away at the keyboard, she reads or watches television. "Since we're in the same room we can share conversations and kisses while doing our own thing," she reports.

God rewards generously those who show mercy and kindness to others.

It works for them. They just increased their BQ. That's what flexibility is all about.

When we respond to change and the challenges it brings with anger and threats and ultimatums, it just makes an already difficult situation worse. With those hastily spoken (shouted?) words can come rifts that may never be mended. And, after all, the priority here is the stability of your marriage.

Change will come, and when it does, you are in control. You choose your response—just as Paula chose hers. "If this is the scenario that needs to be addressed and cared for, then that's what we are going to do—take care of it," she explained of her decision to care for her mother-in-law. "That's part of being responsible. That's part of being a combined family."

When you're very young, you have a lot of learning to do. When you come together as mature people, you know what path you're on.

PAULA

THE PLEASURE OF BENDING

John and Lillian had each been married for over thirty years when their respective spouses died. They say their six-year marriage has been remarkably easy. Why? "We were prepared by experience," John explains. "We both knew the need for give-and-take in a relationship."

They knew how to bend. It sounds simplistic, but a simple shift in your attitude can help you find joy even in challenging situations. Some years ago we got to know a woman in our writing certificate program at Cal State University Long Beach who talked often about her grandmother, the most important person in her life. In time we had the privilege of meeting this grandma and hearing her story.

"Wanda" was an older, never-before-married lady when she married a dashing man with two baby grandchildren. They had not yet celebrated their second anniversary when the children's mother abandoned her little ones, and this woman who had never planned on having to raise children found herself with a two-year-old and a three-year-old. It wasn't her first choice of a lifestyle. It wasn't what she had bargained on. But like a willow, she bent.

The grandfather did a great deal to make his wife's life easier, and the children loved their grandpa. But when they were still young, Grandpa died suddenly of a heart attack, and Wanda was now left with two children to raise alone. She got a job in a beauty shop and worked while the children were in school, but she made it a point to always be home when they got home.

That's unbelievable commitment to children she never bargained for, children who aren't even related to her by birth.

Wanda now says, "You know, at first it seemed like ending up with those kids was such a tragedy for our marriage. But now I look back and I can't imagine life without them. That tragedy turned out to be the greatest joy of my life."

Amazing, isn't it? Every circumstance has the potential for joy.

A friend of ours named Jason tells of the bittersweet joy he found in bending. One of his fondest childhood memories was piling into his Uncle Pete's pickup truck and driving to a nearby Pennsylvania farm to cut down the family Christmas tree. As a thirty-five-year-old newlywed, with a California wife and a five-year-old stepdaughter, he insisted on reprising his childhood tradition. Only now the nearest tree farm was miles away up very winding California roads.

As they zipped past Christmas tree lot after Christmas tree lot filled with beautiful Oregon-grown trees—with his increasingly carsick wife and daughter begging him to stop—Jason drove relentlessly on in his quest for that perfect fresh-chopped tree. The day was a disaster. Even the tree they finally found was crummy-looking. That was fifteen years ago, and they have bought their tree at a Christmas tree lot every year since.

"I know it seems like a very small thing," Jason says, "but it was a painful adjustment for me. It meant giving up a very dear memory. But we have made other memories of our own."

Instead of succumbing to hopelessness or resentment, do what Jason did. Work together to shift your perspective. Move from: "Yikes, look what's happening to us!" to "Hey, look what's happening!" It will make all the difference.

Children's children are a crown to the aged, and parents are the pride of their children.
PROVERBS 17:6

OVERSTRESS

We don't want to sound glib. Many of the unexpected stressors that hit us can be powerful indeed. We know that all too well from personal experience. Sometimes they can even sneak up on you in the form of "too much of a good thing," as happened to Dan several years ago while we were still doing weekend writing classes through various state colleges.

Dan had started consulting for a public seminar company, and although the original understanding was that he would work every other week, their business was so good and he was in such demand as a speaker, they began to ask him to work fill-in weeks as well. The result was a good deal more money, but it also meant sometimes working five weeks in a row before getting a week off the road. Then it would start all over again.

In the seminar business, ten days a month is considered a full load. To go to fifteen or twenty days a month, and to maintain that load for long, is heading for burnout. Add to that the fact that every Saturday and many Sundays we were teaching daylong writing classes somewhere in the state of California. After about six months of that pressure, Dan was ready to crack—and he did one day.

It was a Saturday and Kay and Dan were teaching at a Cal State campus in the Los Angeles area. As she was doing her portion of the class, Dan sat in the back and went over some commission schedules for the previous month that he had received from the seminar company, comparing their figures with the ones he had worked out for himself. Nearly every one of theirs was significantly less than his. Added up, that meant about a thousand dollars less in commissions. It made Dan so angry he snapped. He immediately went outside to find a pay phone and call the general accountant. Because it was a weekend, he got the accountant's voice mail, where he foolishly left a recording of a lot of angry, even abusive remarks.

Only later did it hit Dan that he had been acting out of overstress. He rechecked his figures and realized he had been using the wrong basis for his calculations. Redone, they were almost exactly the same as the company's. He felt like an idiot, but it was too late to cancel the voicemail.

Instead, Dan called the accountant the following Monday and apologized profusely. The man graciously accepted, but the relationship and Dan's reputation were both too damaged to ever be the same. However, the two of them agreed Dan had acted out of character due to stress. Within thirty days Dan was back to working an average of two weeks per month. He says now that he wishes he had had sense enough to ask for a cutback rather than push himself until it was forced on him.

When you get to that so-overstressed-I-can't-make-it-one-more-minute point, take a deep breath and ask yourself

- *Is this going to last forever?* We know, we know, it sure feels like it will. But will it really? Almost certainly the answer is "no." Whatever is happening now, however it impacts your life and your plans as a couple, it is sure to change.

- *Is it the only thing going on in our lives right now?* The answer to this question is always "no." However major and overwhelming the situation that is causing you stress, however upsetting it is to you personally and to your family, there are other things happening as well. Good things. Things that can bring a smile to your face, if only for a moment. Things that bring you pleasure and give you reason to be thankful.

- *Has anyone else ever gone through something like this and come through a better, more joyful person because of it?* The answer to this question is "yes." Always. Whatever your challenge, someone else has faced it and has come through it victorious. And God can bring you through, too.

God shouldn't be the last resort, either. He is the ulti-mate source of power and change. You say you cannot be flexible? You say you cannot bend enough to cope with what

That is the secret of any good marriage, I think: Being the kind of support your spouse needs you to be, while continuing to pursue the things that are important to you (and trusting your spouse will be there to support you when you need it).

ANDREA

has intruded into your life? Here is what the apostle Paul says in Philippians 4:13: "I can do everything through him [Christ] who gives me strength."

TEMPER YOUR INFLEXIBILITY WHILE YOU STILL CAN

Our favorite scene in the movie *The Story of Us* is where the exasperated couple (played by Bruce Willis and Michelle Pfeiffer) is in bed arguing when suddenly each of their four parents appear on the bed alongside them. Soon there are six people arguing, with the two mothers and two fathers doing most of it.

Of course, the parents are not actually there, but their influence is so great, they may as well be. Pretty awful thought—your parents right in bed arguing alongside you— especially because it so often feels true.

But don't just throw your hands in the air and run. That's not going to do any good. We are strong proponents of seizing the moment and making changes while we still can. This is one of the big advantages of getting married when we're over thirty-five, after all. We're the perfect age—old enough to recognize those tell-tale traits of our parents when we look in the mirror (or listen to ourselves when we're angry . . . nagging . . . just being us), but we are still young enough to make changes in ourselves.

Maturity means recognizing that our way is not always the right way. It means coming to know when to hold tight, when to loosen our grip and when to let go.

"I really appreciate Dan's willingness to change roles when the situation calls for it and not to be stressed by it," Kay says. "That's something I have never before seen modeled in a marriage—not by my parents, not by my parents-in-law, not in my first marriage. When I am working hard on

God, give us the serenity to accept what cannot be changed, the courage to change what should be changed, and the wisdom to distinguish the one from the other.

REINHOLD NEIBUHR

IDEA:
Give your partner credit for a job— or a word— well done.

a project, Dan cooks dinner. If Dan is busier than I am, I do it. Whoever doesn't cook does the dishes—unless that person's deadline pressure is too great. If Dan sees that the laundry needs to be done, he does it. It's really nice when we are both working at home not to be fenced in by 'man's work' and 'woman's work.' "

Living, growing, healthy beings change and evolve. It's true of people and it's true of marriages. When problems or difficulties show up, it is crucial that we address them immediately. We can remind each other that our marriage is a work in progress. We are good today but we will be even better tomorrow. With a little time we will be truly great!

One loving heart sets another on fire.

St. Augustine

For Discussion

How much can your relationship weather? Here's a test to help you determine how solid your ground is.

How do I make my spouse feel when things don't go my way?

☐ Like this marriage is more than I bargained for.

☐ Loved, secure and cared for in spite of our difficulties.

What do I do when my spouse is discouraged?

☐ Wait for him or her to get out of the funk; after all, I'm not feeling so great either!

☐ Give an emotional boost.

What about my needs?

☐ Ignore them. It's selfish to think about myself.

☐ Let him or her know what I need. If I don't ask for help now and then, my marriage will grow lopsided and I will become resentful.

Why is God giving us too much?

   ☐ God never gives us more than we can bear.

   ☐ God does give us more than we can bear. Otherwise, we wouldn't need him; but he will always bear us.

First boxes checked? Watch the weather forecast. Those storms could knock your relationship over.

Second boxes checked? Your relationship is on solid ground.

Your Job, My Career

When Doug took Vanessa to the four-star French restaurant in downtown Manhattan to discuss their final pre-marriage arrangements, he had no idea the shock that was in store for him. It started innocently enough. All he said was, "When you move up to my apartment—"

"Hold it!" Vanessa interrupted. "I can't move up to Manhattan!" Doug started to protest that she certainly couldn't stay in her New Jersey house two hours away from him, and *he* certainly couldn't relocate since he worked on Wall Street, but before he could get a word out, she rushed on, "Hey, I work seventy hours a week! I don't have time to commute!"

They sat and stared at each other. What had they been thinking? Doug had just assumed . . . Vanessa had just figured . . .

TWO KEY PERCEPTIONS

Where life-work is concerned, we noted two key perceptions running through the many and varied responses we received. The first is that a career does not automatically have more value than a job, and vice versa. The second is that a career does not always have to produce an income to be considered a career. Couples who share these two perceptions

A job is not a career. I think I started out with a job. It turned into a career and changed my life.

BARBARA WALTERS

seem to have had easier adjustments in merging their lives, values and work. Those who had greater difficulty in accommodating one another's career-and-life decisions apparently did not agree on these perceptions, even though they thought they did.

Therefore, any savvy couple must first analyze their perceptions of careers and their relative values. They must then face the fact that meshing lives and careers almost always means making some concessions as well.

So what are some of these potential "clash areas" that a savvy couple can defuse ahead of time? Here are a few for starters:

- *Understand the givens of your and your spouse's work requirements.* You may not like the fact that your spouse's job requires travel, but if it does, it does no good to badger her about it. You may not like the fact that he has to work Saturdays, but if that is his shift, and he cannot change it—or does not want to—your choices are to adjust to it or have it be a constant clash in your relationship.

  Or consider Anthony and Lynn's dilemma: She could stay in Kentucky where she had a wonderful position teaching in a seminary but where there was nothing on a long-term professional basis for Anthony, or she could go with him to Maine. Anthony says, "From the beginning, that presented a problem in that there was very little for her to teach at the small public university where we were.

  "As we looked down the road, we knew that one option was for her to do a little of this, a little of that— teaching piano part time, adjuncting at the university where I taught, perhaps some independent writing projects. But from the beginning, the limited possibilities in Maine for her made us more open to the possibility of leaving Maine—which, after several years of talking about, we actually did this past summer."

- *Understand that there are many people who are not paid what they are worth, and you or your spouse may be among them.* It is sometimes appropriate and even wise to ask for a raise, and there are times and ways to do so. But to constantly chase money—or to nag your spouse to do so—can have dire consequences both on the job and in the relationship. Many people are not paid what they are worth (including just about every teacher we have ever met) while others are paid way too much. Life isn't fair.

- *Understand that many men feel threatened when their wives earn more than they do.* We know, we know, it shouldn't be this way, but it is a fact. Yet in the year 2000, more than 7.4 million American wives had higher incomes than their husbands—almost double the number in 1981. If there is a disparity in what the two of you bring home, and it favors the wife, be aware that a problem could be brewing.

- *Understand that your spouse isn't the cause of your work stress.* When you are snowed under at work and you come home to find still more that needs to be done, it is easy to turn your weary frustration on each other. Don't allow yourself to lose sight of the focus of your stress. Work stress is work stress. Your spouse doesn't cause it and your spouse cannot make it go away—although he or she can certainly help to ease it some.

Whatever you do, work at it with all your heart, as working for the Lord, not for men.

Colossians 3:23

Whatever your hand finds to do, do it with all your might.

Ecclesiastes 9:10

The FBI's Bureau of Crime Statistics reports that 70 percent of domestic violence occurs during the half-hour "window" during which both working spouses arrive home. Perhaps we need to offer comfort more than seek to be comforted—after all, "what goes around comes around."

CHANGE PERSPECTIVE, CHANGE PERCEPTION

When people ask us what we do for a living, we say, "Kay is a writer who speaks and Dan is a speaker who writes." That just about sums us up.

Nice, glamorous careers, huh? Easy jobs, never have to get our hands dirty. Kay just shlumping around in her bathrobe until noon, eating bonbons and writing when the muse strikes. Dan off to exciting cities, enjoying the applause of enthusiastic crowds, dining afterward on steak and lobster.

What a life! Too bad it never happens. Let's run that by again.

Here's Kay, working 'round the clock. She's under yet another all-too-near deadline. What's she eating? A dinner of popcorn and hot tea, working without sleep so long she starts to hallucinate. As for Dan, he goes to exciting cities, all right, he just never sees anything of them except the airport and the inside of a meeting room. In fact, he has slept in some of the most prestigious airports in the world. As for dinner, don't even say "burger and fries" in his presence.

In addition to a good bit of the glamour being gone, we noticed that with maturity came a new perspective on one's employment. One of our younger respondents told us, "In my twenties, I was career driven and materially needy. Now I've realized that no matter how great a job or how full the wallet, at the end of the day it's relationships that give you the most joy. And if you can find the one and only with whom to share your life, so much the better." Her husband added, "I'm well grounded career-wise, ready to make a lifetime commitment. I wasn't ready for that even at thirty."

That's not to say that a job has to be a career or that a career has to last forever. Things change, and so do we. Dan has had four distinct careers in his life. And during each one, had you asked him if he was planning future career changes, he would undoubtedly have said, "Absolutely not! Why would I?" But each time, the situation changed.

Kay trained for a career that she maintained part time while raising her children. She, too, had no intention of looking toward anything else. But she would never go back to that career. For her, too, things changed.

When Andrea and Scott married, Andrea was working as senior editor for a Christian publishing house. After their marriage, she says, "Something happened I never saw coming. I developed a craving to work from home, just to stay at home as much as possible. This startled both of us, because up to that time I had enjoyed my work a great deal. However, I have returned to school and am enjoying my freelance life."

QUESTION: How many major jobs have you held between you? Which would you classify as careers?

Janet taught kindergarten in Hawaii for ten years. She vowed never to marry a teacher or anyone who lived where it was cold, but she still went ahead and married Peter, a teacher who lived in Boston. She also vowed to keep on teaching, but that also changed.

"Peter and I weren't getting any younger," she said, "and we really wanted to start a family. So I decided not to get a job after all. Instead we began looking into the possibility of adopting. Even so, it took several years before we got our first child and several more before we got our second."

DEALING WITH CHANGE IS HARD ENOUGH ALREADY . . .

There is nothing wrong with change; it is simply a part of life. Unless that change is being forced on one partner by the other. Unless one partner is taking advantage of the other. Unless one partner is demeaning the other. That sort of thing is simply breeding trouble.

Not long ago we ran into a couple downtown. He had been out of work for over a year and was doing consulting out of the house—although we were well aware that they would be very hungry indeed if it weren't for the salary the wife earned. "Give them one of your cards, Dear," the wife said to her husband. "Show them your little business."

Little business? Ouch.

Encourage your partner in the difficulties of the job. And praise a job well done.

Feeling important is important. And it is awfully nice to have others around you who make you feel like you're indispensable. Here's the great side of being a couple: You have a respite at home. Do everything you can to make sure home stays just that for both of you. Make a conscious effort to leave the office behind you (not so easy when your office is right there in the family room!). Focus on the positive aspects of your home life. And make time for those all-important family rituals:

- Have dinner together.

- Enjoy your friends.

- Attend church together.

- Snuggle up together and watch a movie you both enjoy.

STRIKING THAT ELUSIVE BALANCE

Certainly it is the goal of each of us to strike a balance between earnings, benefits, personal satisfaction and career opportunities. Where is that balance? Tough question. For one thing, the balance is different for each couple. And even for a specific couple it can be frustratingly elusive. Case in point:

Andrea and Scott were strongly advised to have Scott find another job that did not require him to work in the family business. But that turned out to be the very advice they did *not* follow.

"We did focus on minimizing the impact of my work," said Scott, "through a more equitable sharing of responsibilities and through establishing better boundaries in the arena of my work and family."

TRAVEL

A business aspect that was a pro to some and a con to others was business travel. The first two years of our marriage, Dan was gone as much as he was home. Kay tried to schedule her intensive round-the-clock writing jags during his absences, but it still was very hard to be apart so much. Because we have no children at home, we were able to sometimes pack up and travel together. Now that Dan travels less often, Kay is even more likely to go along, especially when it is in driving distance. Since a nice hotel is usually part of the deal, we try to arrive early and enjoy the pool and amenities the grounds have to offer. Of course, that isn't possible—or even desirable—for many couples, but for us it is a nice travel perk.

Not everyone saw traveling as a burden.

"I didn't want to live alone, I knew that, and yet I needed some independence," said Sophie. "After forty-four years, if a man said I needed to be home every night for dinner, I couldn't do it." Eight years later, the road no longer looks so good. She actually *does* want to be home every night. Who could know?

"It was hard for me the first year," Sophie admits. "I was glad that when things got tough I had to be gone. It was my issue with privacy. It took me a while to get the concept of being married."

Still, for many couples, being apart can put a great stress on the marriage. It's definitely something that needs to be discussed.

QUESTION:
Could you arrange to give each other a half-hour at the end of the workday, to do with exactly as you and your spouse please? Dinner may have to wait a little longer, but you may enjoy it more after a bubble-bath, or a chance to dabble in your garden, take a little walk. Do a little light reading, go through the mail—in short, whatever you like that relaxes you.

WORK SCHEDULES

I came into the
marriage selfish.
If I wanted to turn
on the television,
I didn't have
to ask anybody.
When I was away I
had my privacy.

SOPHIE

QUESTION:
How do you
manage to preserve
your time together?
Do you make time
together a high
priority—especially
fun time?

One newlywed bride says, "Even though our work schedules are the same as before we were married, they offer continual transitional problems. I work nine-thirty until six, Monday through Friday, but he works from two till midnight Tuesday through Saturday. That means we don't see each other at all Tuesday through Friday and only a few hours on Saturday afternoon and on Monday evening. Sunday is our only full day together."

Talk about scheduling challenges.

"Now that we're married," she adds, "it seems like being apart bothers us even more, especially when we want to do house projects or 'couples' activities."

Sometimes work schedules can be adjusted and sometimes they can't. Even when they can, the preferred schedule isn't always preferred by both spouses. Still, it is very difficult to establish and sustain a healthy marriage when one or both of you have job demands that seem endless. If that is the case, you might do well to ask a counselor to help you carve out an equitable time to ensure that your relationship will be protected.

AN ALTERNATIVE CAREER

So does your endeavor have to earn money in order for it to be considered a true career? On this one we hear a resounding "no." It's coming from stay-at-home moms and dads. It's coming from the woman who works more than a forty-hour week as the teaching leader of Bible Study Fellowship. It's coming from the wife who works full time writing software so that her husband can work full time as an assistant minister for a small church that can afford to pay him only half time. It comes from the wife who works Monday, Wednesday and Friday mornings in the church office as a volunteer, and the man who identifies himself as a scout leader first and as a salesman only as an afterthought.

Maureen, thirty-nine and eight years older than her Mr. Right in 1992, decided on a new career right away. During her years of singlehood, she had done a lot of things—traveled, become financially secure, established a substantial business career. It was all exceedingly satisfying. But when she got married, she turned in her resignation and signed up for a whole new calling: she wanted to be a mother. "We had three children, one right after the other. The love I have for my children knocked me off my feet. I had never felt that kind of love for another person—not even my husband. I would not be truthful if I said I didn't sometimes miss my old career. But I wouldn't trade for anything."

SOLUTIONS

So where are the solutions? Sometimes this juggling of job and career calls for flexibility. In fact, it's amazing just how much flexibility some over-thirty-five couples are willing to build into their marriages in order to incorporate their careers. One couple we'll call Philip and Helen have an especially unique arrangement.

Helen, a long-time high school history teacher in Tucson, Arizona, held off marrying Philip because she had no desire to move to his northern Minnesota farm, and Philip made it perfectly clear to Helen that love and marriage had a whole lot going for it, but the farm held generations of history for him and farming was in his blood. There is a situation that calls for the wisdom of Solomon!

Yet Helen and Philip did marry, and for thirteen years, until Helen retired at fifty-five, they maintained two households, one in Arizona and one in Minnesota. Throughout the school year, Helen lived in Tucson. As soon as school was

Do you see a man skilled in his work? He will serve before kings.

PROVERBS 22:29

Because I was older I had enough experience so that I didn't feel I was missing out on anything. I saw my friends who were divorced—some divorced many times. They had gotten married very young, and there was a whole life they never had. I had done all that.

SOPHIE

out in June, her bags were packed and she was overjoyed to leave the desert heat for the cool of a northern summer on the farm. She stayed there, raising her garden and getting things ready for the state fair, but came back in time to get her classroom ready for fall. Philip stayed on after Helen left, but when the crops were in, he headed for Arizona where he spent the winter basking in the desert sun. He stayed until it was time for spring planting. Then he went back to Minnesota and awaited Helen's arrival in June.

"So you see," Helen said, "we actually *spend* more time together than most couples do!"

Now that they are retired, they travel together between their two homes, Minnesota from Easter to October and Arizona from October to Easter.

It's amazing what can work when you are dedicated to each other and to supporting each other's goals. There generally are more options than at first appear. And at this point in your life, there are more reasons than ever to search them out. As Russell so wisely observed, "I now have a lot less to prove in life for myself. My ambitions and my drive are much more realistic—more conducive to a satisfactory marriage. For example, I am now much more focused on building a relationship than on building a career."

The great thing in this world is not so much where we are, but in what direction we are moving.

OLIVER WENDELL HOLMES

FOR DISCUSSION

From where you both are now—in a paying career, working at home, retired—write up a joint mission statement of where you see the value of your time and efforts, and where you would like to be five, ten or fifteen years down the road.

Yikes!
We've Got a Family!

"Meeting Greg was like a fairy tale," said Diana, forty-eight, in a soft Southern drawl. "He was my knight in shining armor come to rescue me from my horrible childhood and disastrous first marriage. Greg is an architect, and he lived with his two children in a beautiful home he had designed. Five-year-old David seemed like a miniature adult but three-year-old Ruthanne was still in diapers. The year before, Greg's wife had deserted the family—one day she just up and left. I should have been scared at the thought of an instant family, but instead I was intrigued. And I was foolish enough to believe I could simply step in and become the princess bride of this fairy tale."

Diana's fairy tale didn't even make it intact to the wedding.

"Greg wasn't spending enough time with me," she says. "We couldn't even have a proper date. It was always the children, the children, the children."

Still, Diana told herself not to worry. Once they were married, everything would be fine.

It wasn't. And day by day her jealousy grew. "Many times I felt like I was an outsider looking in," she says. "The chil-

Sixty-five percent of all remarriages involve children from prior marriages and thus form stepfamilies.

STEPFAMILIES
ASSOCIATION OF
AMERICA

dren and Greg were connected in a way I wasn't. They had been a family longer."

Still, Diana was determined to be a good mother to David and Ruthann and it annoyed her to no end that Greg was so laid-back when it came to discipline. "We're going to end up with a couple of spoiled brats on our hands!" she would exclaim in exasperation. She knew how to lay down the law!

Three years later, when David was eight and Ruthanne was starting first grade, the children's biological mother reappeared in Nashville and stepped back into their lives. She didn't want the children to live with her and cramp her style, but she did enjoy showering them with fun and gifts and a rules-free lifestyle every other weekend, except when she decided not to show up.

Demographers predict that stepfamilies will be the most common type of family in the USA by the year 2010.

MARY ANN ARONSOHN, MARRIAGE, FAMILY AND CHILD THERAPIST

Unfortunately—and with the best of intentions—Diana set about trying to counter both the indulgent "real" mother and the kids' too-easy dad in exactly the wrong ways. Before she knew it, she had become the epitome of the classic "wicked stepmother." Her and Dad's house was strict and boring and had long lists of rules, while Mom's house was fun with new toys and anything-goes abandon. Diana didn't know how to be flexible, and Greg didn't know how to discipline lovingly.

"It was a disastrous set of dynamics, to be sure," says Diana, reflecting back on those desperate days. "But the worst thing of all was that I knew the biggest problem was inside me. I *could not* love those children. I was so angry, so miserable, so exhausted, I just wanted out. . . . But I also wanted to be with Greg. And I did want to be able to love the children. So I cried out to God. I admitted that my *magna cum laude* degree in psychology and all my years of counseling hadn't done one thing to equip me for loving two broken little children."

Today, blended families are a fact of life, especially for many of the couples who marry over the age of thirty-five. And the fact is, however you plan, however earnest and noble your intentions, when you bring others along into a new situation that changes their lives so drastically, to a greater or lesser degree, there will be adjustments for everyone.

STEPFAMILY BAGGAGE

Put "step" in front of words like *mother* or *father* or *child* and almost everyone suddenly has an unrealistic expectation. Little wonder. That one short word lugs along a heavy load of fearful expectations. Either we think of mean old stepmothers from Cinderella and Snow White legend, or we think of saintly Julie Andrews in *The Sound of Music*. No one wants to be the wicked one, but who can live up to Maria Von Trapp? And as for stepfathers, how many can truly form the immediate loving bonds we expect from them? And if they do, how can they handle the rejection that so often comes from trying too hard too quickly?

We were fortunate that on our wedding day, Dan's wise son, Toby—who was our best man—said to us, "Let's never use the word *step* in our family." And we haven't. We have left it up to the kids to call us what they want—by our first names generally, "Mom" or "Dad" occasionally.

Of course, it has been easier for us because we were both widowed. Our children don't feel pulled between two sets of parents. Also, our children are grown and out on their own. Still, whatever the details of how it comes together, a blended family is different from a birth family. And looking at some of those differences might help us understand how to deal with them more effectively.

- **Stepfamilies come together as the result of a major loss in the family.** Whatever the cause—death, divorce,

The word "step" comes from the Old English word "steop," which meant "bereaved"; a stepchild then was understood to be an orphan.

MARY ANN ARONSOHN

Approximately 25 percent of all children in the U.S. live in a stepfamily.

STEPFAMILIES
ASSOCIATION OF
AMERICA

abandonment—there has been a loss. The parents may be so overjoyed to find each other and to love again that they cannot understand how their children are feeling in the depths of their souls.

One of our over-thirty-five "new" husbands knows this from experience. "Sally had been widowed over two years when we first met, and her time had been focused mainly on her two boys," he said. "So when she started spending time with me, they felt jealous of me because now I was getting their mother's attention. It made her feel guilty and me feel bad."

- **They had each other before they had you.** Like it or not, that old bond predates the new bond, and it can't be matched overnight, or in a month or even in a year.

    "Trying to merge all five of our kids and having them come out okay has been our greatest challenge," says Sally. "My oldest is almost grown, and his youngest is just going through potty training. But the hardest hit were my youngest and his oldest who went from being my baby and his big girl to being just the middle kids."

- **The relationship is instant.** One day you are childless and the next you are a parent. Instead of working your way up, you have instant teens. One day you are independent, the next day you are responsible for someone else. You may know it's coming, but you don't grow into it like a birth family does.

- **It's like a marriage all around.** Everyone has to work together, from different sides, from various perspectives and ways of doing things, to make it work. It's more like a marriage cooperative than like a boss giving orders.

- **They're yours, then they aren't.** Often today children

move back and forth between parents. Rules and expectations are different in the two homes. Your rules aren't their rules, and their rules aren't your rules. And kids are quick to pick up on uncertainties and play one against the other.

- **There are others to deal with.** One of the reasons stepfamilies can be so difficult is that there are so many other people that must be dealt with. There are those other parents with whom stepparents are continually compared. Yes, even if those others have died or were abusive or abandoned the family. Memory, or imagination, can be even more powerful than reality.

Sally knows this all too well. When her boys would ask her, "How can you replace Dad with *him?*" she simply acknowledged, "You're right, he is nothing like your father. However, he is also everything your father wasn't. He's a completely different person. That's not a good thing or a bad thing, it's just different."

Then there are the "other parents" who are not always reasonable people with everyone's greatest good foremost in their minds. Just ask Mark, who was somewhat naive and idealistic when yanked into stepfamily life at age forty-two. "For me, the hardest part of stepparenting by far was dealing with Christopher, Rebecca's ex-husband. We went through deeply disturbing problems with his jealousy and possessive attitudes toward Allison, his daughter who was now my stepdaughter. The tension grew and grew until it peaked when another parent accused him of molesting Allison and her friend while they were at his house. In the end, no charges were filed, but the questions and suspicions remain to this day."

Yet that "other father" remains a part of their life. Mark and Rebecca have no choice. The court says so.

I love my dad and I love my mom. But I can't tell my dad I love Mom or he will feel bad, and I can't tell Mom I love Dad or she will feel bad. I have to pretend I only love the one I'm with and that I only like the other one.

LILY, AGE EIGHT; FROM *THE FAMILY PUZZLE*

Of course there are many others who have positive stories to tell of their relationships with the "other parent." Between them, Tom and Kimberly have five teenagers: a thirteen-year-old boy; two girls, fifteen; a seventeen-year-old girl; and a boy, eighteen. Tom's two children, the thirteen-year-old and one of the fifteen-year-olds, live with them half the time. The rest of the time they live two blocks away with Tom's ex-wife, her new husband and their five-year-old, Annie.

How do they all get along? Quite well, actually. "We're all adults and we are all decent people," says Tom. "And we've made a decision to act like it."

They do it so well that Tom's ex-wife and her husband have named Kimberly and Tom in their will as their choice to raise Annie should anything happen to them. "They want her to grow up surrounded by family," says Kimberly. "That's how it should be."

Certainly Kimberly and Tom are an exception. Still, Tom's words ring true: if we are adults, if we are decent people, let us act like it.

Paula observes, "When you're not dealing with mature people, the damage just goes on and on like pebbles in a stream."

IS THERE HOPE?

Hope rests right there with the two of you. The first and most important thing you can do to ensure the success of your blended family is to build a solid relationship between the two of you.

As Dan knows only too well from hard experience: "If you as a couple are not in agreement, stepchildren can quickly drive a wedge between you. They will pick up on your fundamental differences and exploit them if they choose to.

Do you want to know the secret to successful partnership parenting? Here it is: STICK TOGETHER— ALWAYS.

NANCY AND BILL PALMER, *THE FAMILY PUZZLE*

Dear friends, let us love one another, for love comes from God.

1 JOHN 4:7

"For example, I felt we should lock up the house at midnight, even if some of the older kids weren't in by then. My second wife would not back me on this, however, because her kids would frequently lose their house keys and raise a ruckus to get in at one or two a.m. Rather than encourage our young adults to be home earlier, or to become more responsible with their keys, she insisted we leave the house unlocked all night for them. I could never adjust to this, especially since her house had been burgled twice before we were married.

"But she would take her kids' side in this, fighting about it with me rather than facing their combined opposition. They were just too used to having it their way and weren't about to give in and make room for a changed situation."

And it doesn't even have to be intentional on the part of the children.

One of our respondent couples found themselves arguing more and more about issues that had to do with their kids. As those arguments grew in frequency, they also grew in intensity. The children, already insecure because of the losses they had suffered, grew more and more fearful that there was going to be another divorce and they were going to lose yet again. The two parents didn't realize how devastating their arguments were until one especially explosive altercation ended with a child frighteningly panicked.

"That was a wake-up call to both of us," the husband told us. "We vowed to never again let ourselves lose control, and we never, ever fight in front of the children. Of course, the kids can always tell when something's wrong between us, and we take the time to explain that we're working out a problem, that it doesn't mean we don't love each other and that we certainly aren't going to get a divorce. We don't want to shelter them so much that they grow up in a fantasy

Having family responsibilities and concerns just has to make you a more understanding person.

SANDRA DAY O'CONNOR, SUPREME COURT JUSTICE

world, believing that parents never argue or that there's something wrong with them if they do.

"The main thing is, that whole nasty experience taught us we *must* stop and try to see each other's point of view. This has made an incredible difference in our relationship as well as in our relationship with our children and our step-children."

QUESTION:
If you and your spouse were to agree to have a personal date night once a week, what would you do?

See the progression? *The couple's* relationship first. Unless you dedicate special time and attention to your own relationship, the foundation upon which you build will be weak. That makes it far more difficult to support the subsequent weight of your family.

You may well be thinking, *we have no time together. Our schedules make it impossible.* We understand your dilemma, but the consequences of neglecting your primary relationship are far too grave. You have to change your thinking from "we can't afford to," to "we can't afford *not* to." And actually, it's not *that* hard or time-consuming.

Some couples swear by a date night once a week. Others get up early on Saturday morning to watch the sun rise together, or go for an evening walk around the neighborhood once a week, or sit together in the living room and talk for an hour one night a week, after everyone else is in bed. The thing is to find something that will work for you and then *do* it.

NOT EVERYONE HAS THE SAME NEEDS

Several of the families we talked to had some variation of this scenario: "We tried having family night together on Friday nights with games and popcorn and movies until midnight. The little kids loved it, but the older kids never want to come. What's wrong?"

What's wrong? Teenagers don't want to spend Friday night hanging out with their family, that's what's wrong.

And it puts them in a really difficult position having to choose between you and the school football game with their friends.

It's really important that you find a way to address the different needs of the members of your blended family, both by their ages and development, and also by their personalities. An outgoing child will be much different from a quiet, private child. The other relationships in your kids' lives will also make a difference.

A couple wrote to advice columnist Ann Landers stating that they were planning to get married and, in order to help blend their families of children in their late teens and early twenties, decided to take everyone to Europe. Problem is, one son moved up the date of his own wedding so he could bring his bride along despite an agreement not to include anyone else, and if he couldn't bring her, he announced, he wouldn't come. The other kids resented it, the stepdad didn't feel he could afford the extra expense, the mom didn't want her son to stay home, and everyone was frustrated and stressed. What to do? Leave the son at home? Give in and spring for the new couple's expenses? Insist the son come and leave his new bride home? Cancel the trip and forget the whole thing?

Ann suggested allowing the new couple to come but telling them they would have to either split up (there was going to be one room for the girls and one for the boys) or pay for their own accommodations. Good solution, considering this young woman is also going to be a part of the family— blended in through marriage to the son.

You are forming a new family together, and it is important to get to know one another. Doing fun things together is a good way to do that, although starting out with stress built in is unfortunate. When you are dealing with older kids, it's a good idea to ask for their input.

Stepchildren always add challenges with their split loyalties and immaturity.

CLIFFORD

By letting [our children] see us as we really are, we are teaching them to glide out their own glitches.

NANCY AND BILL PALMER, *THE FAMILY PUZZLE*

Dealing with Special Challenges

If you ask John and Lillian what the biggest challenge to their marriage has been, they will answer in unison, "Jeremy!"

Jeremy is Lillian's grown son who suffers from schizophrenia. In dealing with this young man, John is sensible, businesslike and, in most cases, rational. He knows it is important to give to Jeremy, but not so much that it cripples him. He understands that Jeremy needs to be permitted a degree of freedom, but he must not be allowed to take over.

Let us not love with words or tongue but with actions and in truth.

1 John 3:18

That's all well and good for John. But Lillian is Jeremy's mother. All the sensibilities and reasoning and businesslike approaches in the world don't do a thing to satisfy the deep maternal hurt she feels when she sees her son in distress, nor do they relieve the pangs of guilt that periodically overwhelm her.

Before they married, one of John's friends took him aside and said, "I know you love Lillian, and this is all wonderful for you. But do you comprehend the size of the challenge here? Do you realize what it means to take on her schizophrenic son?"

John told him, "Yes, I know. And it's worth it." Of course John didn't know, but looking back he still says it's worth it.

Be Patient—with Everyone

Dave was forty-two and a lifelong bachelor when he and Karen married. Suddenly he was not only sharing his previously quiet one bathroom home in the Wisconsin woods with a wife, but also with her eleven-year-old daughter and a puppy they were given for a wedding gift.

From the beginning of their life together, Dave let Karen know that he wanted her to be a stay-at-home wife. In fact, he was ready for semi-retirement himself. Karen agreed, but she was frustrated cooped up in that old house that needed so much work. For his part, Dave found it hard to give up the freedom to come and go whenever he liked that he had always enjoyed. Also, he felt awkward around Karen's daughter, Hannah. He had no idea what his role with her should be. As for Hannah, she didn't like Dave one bit and she let him know it as only a determined eleven-year-old can.

Dave was fortunate that Hannah wasn't a full-fledged teenager, or their problems may well have been even greater. The older children are when you set out to blend them, and the more traumatic the loss they endured, the longer and harder it will be for them to settle into a comfortable new relationship. For older children, think in terms of years rather than months. Be patient. In addition to spending time together as a family, you can help by having each parent spend individual time with each child, sharing an experience together. The goal here is to begin to build a family history together.

Let the little children come to me, and do not hinder them, for the kingdom of God belongs to such as these.

JESUS, IN MARK 10:14

Now grown and married with a family of her own, Hannah feels quite close to Dave and includes him in her life every bit as much as she does her mother.

Regardless of how each person came into your family, reassure each one that there is a special place in the family that only he or she can fill. Then prove it by your actions. One important way to do this is to control the words that come from your mouth. Here are some supportive, positive things you can say to your kids:

- "Whatever differences we have, all of us—your parents and your stepparents—love and care about you."

- "We will never leave you."

- "You are a very important part of our family."

- "I really, really like spending time with you."

• "As you grow, your schedule will change, but you will always be an important part of our family."

The need for patience isn't limited to the children who live with you—even part time.

"The hardest thing for us was dealing with a very angry ex-wife who thoroughly poisoned my husband's daughter against her father and me," said one of our respondents. "I didn't even know him when they were going through their divorce—and I'm so glad I didn't! But in her mind I'm still the one who took him away. And now she figured he had two new children he could love and cherish so he didn't need this daughter any longer. She played so many games that were so bad, and she still is eighteen years later. How could a mother do this to her child?"

Patience.

Love is patient.
1 CORINTHIANS 13:4

During his last four years, Kay's first husband Larry lived at a nearby care facility, and Kay would visit him almost daily. If she happened to be there on a Friday, she would always see an elderly man named Ben. They eventually struck up a friendship and she came to know what a kind and caring man Ben is.

Ben had been divorced from his alcoholic first wife for ten years. Now she was institutionalized in the care facility with severe mental problems. Yet every week Ben was there visiting her. When Kay asked him why he continued to come, he said, "Because she has no one but me. I'm her only visitor, her only connection with the outside world and her former life. I know my new wife wishes I didn't, but she doesn't say too much."

Patience.

"For a year and a half Paula cared for my mother who was growing more and more feeble," said Clifford.

Patience. Patience. Patience.

SET REALISTIC BOUNDARIES

Marriage and family counselor Mary Ann Aronsohn, whose expertise is as a stepfamily therapist, emphasizes the importance of staying aware that each stepfamily member has basic needs.

- The *stepparent* needs to feel accepted and not so much of an outsider.

- The *parent* needs to stay connected with his or her own children.

- The *children* need to feel some sense of control and be able to express their feelings of loss.

- *Everyone* needs to build a home that will eventually feel comfortable, familiar, predictable and satisfying.

Many of the families we talked to spoke of the differences in their parenting styles. Greg and Diana, whom we met at the beginning of the chapter, were an extreme example. Greg—laid back and easygoing to a fault—loved to play with the children and indulge them. So what if they ate in the living room and spilled food on the carpet? Carpet is just to walk on anyway! So what if they had ice cream before dinner and wouldn't eat their meat loaf and green beans? Hey, you're only a kid once. Diana, on the other hand, was so legalistic that she came across as downright unloving.

Mark came into stepparenting with a different perspective. Like Diana, he had married into parenthood. But unlike Diana, Mark stood back and, after some initial clashes, made it a point to be the support person rather than the primary parent. "I was well aware of how critical it was to agree on parenting styles," Mark said. "So I watched Rebecca to see what her style was. We had our differences but she, like

Train a child in the way he should go, and when he is old he will not turn from it.

PROVERBS 22:6

me, was a believer in firm discipline done in love, not in hate or anger."

Therapist Mary Ann Aronsohn states that attempting to discipline stepchildren before a firm bond and has been developed is likely to backfire. "Let the biological parent do the disciplining," she advises. "The stepparent can help enforce the parent's rules." What if the biological parent isn't around and a situation arises that requires discipline? "Then the stepparent can say, 'I am making sure your mom's (dad's) rules are being followed.'"

One thing all the experts agree on is that stepparents are wise to not discipline stepchildren before a warm, strong bond has developed.

MARY ANN ARONSOHN

DO WHAT HAS TO BE DONE

From the time he began dating Rebecca, Mark was pulled into the bullying tactics of her ex-husband, Christopher. Christopher and his attorney friend used any possible excuse to drag Rebecca into court. The result of one such appearance was court-ordered weekly sessions with a mediator. Problem was, the mediator had totally lost control of the sessions and Christopher used the time to verbally attack Rebecca. Each session ended with her in tears and Christopher smugly gloating. Over the next four years things went from bad to worse as he grew more and more bold, pushing the boundaries in every way possible. Finally he announced he was filing for full custody of Allison.

"I'd had it," Mark recalls. "It was time to counter sue and get Christopher out of the driver's seat."

Mark didn't like doing it, but for everyone's good—Rebecca's, his own and, most of all, Allison's—it had to be done. With Rebecca's encouragement and agreement, Mark had moved from stepparent-observer to the responsible father figure Allison needed so badly in her young life. He had assumed his proper role as her protector, until a time when she became able to fend for herself.

ESTABLISH NEW FAMILY TRADITIONS

Because Kay was always big on family traditions, she and her kids had lots of them that they held dear. For Dan, traditions were not as emphasized. So our challenge was to begin to build a sense of "us" without wiping out the cherished old ways of Kay's family. Gradually we have started finding new routines and rituals of our own.

For instance, Christmas has always been a highly celebrated holiday for Kay's family and also for us. But Kay's first husband never put up Christmas lights. Dan does put up the lights—every year, and on more of the house than the year before. On the night he puts them up, Kay cooks his favorite dinner—chicken and dumplings—to reward his good work.

Now Dan has started doing an extra job decorating the patio with lights. No one can see it from outside, but from Kay's desk those lights are beautiful. It's a special Christmas gift just for Kay. Her kids see what he does and comment on it. They say, "He really loves you!"

Whatever family tradition you establish, it doesn't have to be fancy or elaborate or once a year, like putting up Christmas lights on the house. In fact, the more simple and inexpensive the tradition is, the more likely you can all enjoy it, and more often.

Three of Lillian and John's five grown children live close to them in Missouri. Still, it's not the same as it was when John lived with one of his daughters and he saw all of his girls frequently.

"They love their dad a lot," Lillian says, "and they miss being with him as often as before. So they and their dad meet for breakfast and a long visit at a restaurant every month or so." It's a new family tradition that meets a new circumstance in their life.

They still celebrate birthdays together, but now there are

Leave a legacy for your children by teaching them to care for needy children around the world.

QUESTION:
Do you read the Scriptures together as a family?
Do you give your children a chance to ask questions about your faith?
Do you tell them what God has done in your life?

twice as many of them and twice as many birthdays. And when they get together for holidays, now both families are included.

Accept the Shifts in the Makeup of Your Family

Stepfamilies are not like other families. In stepfamilies kids move back and forth, and people come and go. Sometimes you're alone and sometimes you're not. Sometimes you have a say in the matter at hand and sometimes you don't. It can all be very anxiety provoking.

On Mother's Day, Dan took his three favorite moms to dinner: Kay, his daughter Sara, and his first wife's mother, Margaret. When the waiter came over he said, "Hi there! Are you all a family?"

As one, we answered, "Yes!"

That family could have also included Kay's mother Marjorie; Kay's first husband's mother, Clara; and Kay's daughter, Lisa. They are also all women of our immediate family. And we all feel comfortable together.

Keep in mind that when we blend our families, we blend more than just parents and children. We also bring in our aunts, uncles, brothers, sisters, nephews, nieces—in short, the entire extended family. Though they may not spend as much time with us as our immediate family nor share a home with us, we would be short sighted to ignore the impact our relatives and in-laws can also have on our new lives. And that includes those important people we call our "in-laws-once-removed"—the relatives of our first spouses. They are our children's grandparents and aunts and uncles and cousins, and people who have played an important part in our respective lives. They, too, are a part of the blending process.

Janet already spoke of her adjustment to the impact Pe-

Don't tell me bad things about Mommy. I don't want to hear it.

Molly, age six,
The Family Puzzle

Give it up! Give up trying to control what goes on in your child's other household. As they say in Codependents Anonymous, "Sweep your own side of the street."

Mary Ann Aronsohn

ter's large Irish family had on her. Andrea has had to make her own adjustments to Scott's smaller but equally vociferous family.

"There was one expectation that required significant adjustment during the first two years of our marriage," Andrea explained. "Scott's family is significantly better off financially than mine, and they are also in much closer proximity. Also our approach to money and family time is worlds apart. This made for problems during our first couple of years. But gradually they have come to respect who I am, and I have come to appreciate their point of view on most issues—and to accept the rest as something I am not likely to change."

STILL AND ALL . . .

Mark will be the first to say that having to go through years of stress and counseling was not what he expected of stepparenting. But for him, they were reality. "Adding more children to your family by marriage is not simply more work," he says. "It's a complete change of lifestyle."

One thirty-eight-year-old mother who participated in our survey has had an even more difficult experience to sort out, though she's in a much better place now. Kate (not her real name) was married for six years to a man who beat her regularly. Her daughter remembers those days all too well. She was five when her mommy roused her in the middle of the night and they ran for their lives. When Kate remarried three years ago, she worried a lot about how her daughter would adjust.

"The transition has really been good," she reports. "Michael has accepted my daughter as his own, although with a little trepidation. Last month when he adopted her he was caught off guard when the judge asked if he realized that adopting her meant he'd have to support her—no matter

Many remarried couples conclude upon the first months that their marriage is failing, when, in fact, studies have shown that the estimated time it takes to adapt to being a stepfamily ranges from two to seven years.

DRS. LES AND LESLIE PARROTT, *SAVING YOUR SECOND MARRIAGE BEFORE IT STARTS*

Sons are a heritage from the LORD, children a reward from him.

PSALM 127:3

what—until the age of eighteen. But he paused only briefly before he said, 'Of course!'"

And what of Diana and Greg between then and now?

"Three years into our marriage, by God's grace, we found a new church, and the learning and the healing began," says Diana. "Two books were especially helpful: *When You're Mom No. 2*, by Dr. Beth E. Brown, and *Resolving Conflict in the Blended Family*, by Tom and Adrienne Frydenger. The second book helped especially by dealing with the extremely complicated and painful area of conflicting loyalties.

"We also began to have counseling from someone who was impartial and well trained at helping families. God brought friends to us who were compassionate and wise and didn't just tell us what we wanted to hear. And I was desperate enough to listen to them. It didn't happen easily, and God knows we are far from perfect. But we did become a family. I grew to really love those children and they grew to love and respect me. Yes, we had our problems, but we really did become a family."

Your road to a successful blended family will be different from ours, and it will be different from Diana and Greg's, and from Kate and Michael's, and from Mark and Rebecca's. That's because you aren't any of us and your family is different from all of ours. Each one of us is unique, and each of our families will be blended uniquely. For some of us, we will end up with a family relationship of true friendship. For others, it will be deep love. For some it will be merely mutual tolerance. But . . .

- Step forward with confidence.

- Forget what you think you are supposed to be creating with this family.

I never managed to set aside couples' 'special time' before I entered a stepfamily. Now I see Friday afternoons with Tom as the 'glue' that holds us all together.

MARY ANN ARONSOHN

- Forget the timeline others have worked out for you.

- Understand that the road is not always a smooth one.

- Realize it requires careful attention and dedication.

Get ready for some extremely satisfying relationships. You *are* a real family!

FOR DISCUSSION

List each member of your blended family by name. Next to each name, write one thing you can do to show that person he or she is important to your family.

Don't worry; in a decade or two, all your loving integrity and "doing the right thing" will pay off.

MARY ANN ARONSOHN

Name:
You're important because:

Name:
You're important because:

Name:
You're important because:

Name:
You're important because:

Name:
You're important because:

So What Stuff
Is Big Enough to Sweat?

Maybe you think your life would be wonderful and your marriage would be so much better if only you could get your spouse to shape up on a few matters. It's not all that much to ask, you think. Besides, they're just so irritating. Yet despite your best efforts nothing changes.

- When you go out, you like to show up early ("*Maybe we can give the hostess a hand*"), but your dear spouse drags and drags until you end up arriving late ("*No way am I going to waste my time standing around waiting on someone else!*").

- Your spouse is a penny-pincher ("*Waste not, want not!*") while you are the picture of generosity ("*Hey, it's only money!*").

- That reasonable person you dated suddenly expects an accounting from you for everything. ("*What? You're telling me I have to ask your permission before I buy anything?*")

- When vacation time rolls around, your dear one always pulls out the old sleeping bag and camping gear ("*I thought we'd go up to the cabin for the entire two weeks this year, Hon!"*) while you are still poring hopefully over brochures for luxury cruises (*"Since you like the water so much . . ."*).

"Don't sweat the small stuff!" everyone glibly advises. But what exactly does that mean? Which things are big enough that we *should* sweat them? Can we really just shrug off all those "little" things that make our lives so uncomfortable? Even the tiniest of them have a bad habit of growing until they are completely unrecognizable and out of hand.

Kay recalls, "When I was a young girl a family in our church got a divorce. It was shocking beyond words because divorces were not nearly so common back then, especially among church couples. But the most shocking thing of all was that the stated reason for their divorce was that the husband consistently—are you ready for this?—hung the hangers in his closet backward, with the hook pointing outward rather than inward."

Surely a whole lot of battles had been waged in that house before that fateful decision to divorce was made. Without a doubt there were many angry words spoken, many hurtful things said, many spiteful things done. Yet the thing that was remembered and cited at the divorce proceedings was the way the hangers were hung in the closet. That little thing must have rankled the wife for years and years.

But, you may say, "I can't let every irritation go or in time I will end up resenting my spouse."

True. It is vital that you not stuff a seething small thing down inside you and allow it to burn a hole in your spirit. If you do, that wound will become infected and will fester, and in time it may help destroy your marriage. But stuffing something down is an entirely different thing from making a conscious decision that something is not worth the emotional

I try to put things in perspective. When Sophie gets overexcited, I say, "Let's not major in the minors."

RUSSELL

energy it will cost to worry about it; it is not worth the wear and tear on your marriage.

As one good friend told me, marriage is not 50-50, it's 100-100.

PETER

When contemplating their chances of achieving a long and happy marriage, one newlywed middle-aged couple look to their own parents as examples. His have been married almost forty-five years and have, he says, "endured trials and tribulations, good times and bad, yet they stayed married." She, whose own parents have been married for forty-one years, adds, "I have noted that happy couples work to accept each other's faults and focus on the good rather than the bad."

Paula and Cliff say, "Some things are just too insignificant to even worry about," and then they add, "this may be something you learn from being married previously."

They are right in that some things just aren't worth fighting about, and a prior marriage can be an effective teacher of this. One of Dan's fellow speakers would often tell his seminar attendees, "If you attempt to 'cure' your spouse of some little shortcoming often enough—no matter how lovingly—I can guarantee one thing for sure: you *will* end up with a very interesting 'first marriage.'"

On the other hand, you don't have to be previously married to figure this out. Dan's first in-laws, Margaret and Roy, knew this perfectly well. They were married to one another for almost fifty years, until Roy died of cancer. When Dan or Susan would get into a snit over some truly minor issue, either Margaret or Roy would take them aside, ask what the problem was, listen carefully and then say, "You know, I don't think this is really worth all the fuss you're making. Why don't you save all that energy for something that will actually make a difference?"

It wasn't often easy to admit they were right, but they were. And Susan and Dan were always better off when they took that advice, kissed and made up, and got on with life.

Unfortunately, though, too many people get married repeatedly and never learn this. And here is something else to consider: when you make a big deal over all of the small irritations, what are you doing to the rest of the family? Look at the warning of Proverbs 11:29 as it reads in the Living Bible: "The fool who provokes his family to anger and resentment will finally have nothing worthwhile left." Pretty harsh words!

The husband in the couple we know who learned not to "lose it" in front of the kids was no fool about little things. "Our family grew really quickly with her two and my three," he said. "With five kids I tried to latch onto that control, and control everybody every minute of the day. It drove everyone crazy. I've learned not to stress the small stuff. Since I learned that, my life has been a lot simpler. Little things are little things, and you don't need to hold onto them all."

ASKING FOR CHANGE

How might a spouse express an opinion and ask for change without coming across as a complainer and a nag? When asking for a change in a specific behavior, put your focus on how you are making your spouse feel. Ask yourself:

- Am I setting up a debit and payback system here? If so, drop it. (Bad idea: "You owe me this because last week I . . .")

- Is my tone accusatory, demanding or judgmental? If so, close my mouth in mid-sentence. (Bad idea: "It is so rude to be late! I won't be a part of such boorish behavior!")

- Can we compromise? Now we've got it! Keep it up! (Good idea: "We don't have to be the first ones there. . How about if we arrive at 7:15?")

A marriage is like working together to weave a piece of cloth. You each bring a whole collection of unique threads,

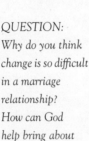

QUESTION:
Why do you think change is so difficult in a marriage relationship? How can God help bring about needed changes in your lives?

but you have to work together to make a pattern—one on the woof and one on the warp. If you don't work together, you won't have enough fabric to hold onto. You'll simply be left hanging in tatters.

And so you start out, slowly at first, very carefully. As you catch on, you fall into step with one another. Just when you think you've got a rhythm going, along come the thread clippers. Minor hassles . . . snip! Frustrations . . . snip! Irritations . . . snip!

Socks left on the floor . . . snip! Toothpaste squeezed in the middle . . . snip! Bed left unmade . . . snip! Phone messages played but not written down . . . snip! The same thing done three days in a row! Snip! Snip! Snip!

By contrast, a wonderfully woven four-decades-old piece of marriage cloth, such as our newlywed couple witnessed in their parents, is a truly magnificent thing to behold. It takes a great deal of work, and a great deal of working together, to achieve such a thing of beauty.

Learning to let go of seemingly inconsequential things is no small part of weaving the cloth of marriage. In so doing, you will begin to discover new ways to nurture each other. That, in turn, will lead to a strengthening of your love.

LEARNING TO LET GO

So, how do you go about letting go of the small stuff? Here are some strategies to help you.

1. **Throw out the scorecard.** We know, this may be the fifth (or the fiftieth) time you've picked up those socks, turned off the bedroom light or put the milk back in the refrigerator. But, really, has keeping your running tally done you any good so far? It obviously hasn't solved the problem. And it certainty hasn't gained you any grati-

QUESTION:
What causes the
snips in your fabric?
Are there some
minor but damaging
issues you are
willing to let go of?

tude or appreciation from your spouse. You never gain the points you expect from keeping score. Sure, it impresses *you*. But when you are reminded of your burden, you just feel that much angrier and more taken advantage of. Those feelings are not lost on your spouse. But instead of feeling guilty and repentant—as you were hoping—your spouse pulls out his or her own score card, and you can be sure you are not going to fare very well on it. Keeping score in a marriage *always* backfires.

2. Recognize your own quirks. We know you'll find this hard to believe, but we do have quirks of our own. Kay has stashes of chocolate stored all over the house. Dan has a weakness for silly greeting cards and he buys them by the handful. Kay has a specific nesting routine she goes through once the light is off at night. Dan is fussy about having the dishwasher loaded just so. We all have quirks. So when you are bothered by your partner's peculiarities, ask yourself, *Is my spouse the odd one for what he or she is doing, or am I the odd one for being bothered by it?*

3. Take pleasure in each other's quirks. Some of the quirkiest things are the very things that become our partner's most endearing traits in time. Anthony's quirk is that he doesn't wear a watch regularly. When he gets excited about a project he's working on, he forgets all about mealtimes, bedtimes, family time—everything. Lynn is struggling to find this endearing. Anthony is struggling to adjust to being a family man.

4. Forget about changing your spouse. As we saw in chapter one, even the most astute among us sometimes goes into marriage thinking, "Well, I know you can't change another person, but once she sees how much more sense

The only good advice is the kind that's asked for. You can say to your spouse, "Look, I have an opinion or some thoughts about this if you're interested in hearing them." But you have to be prepared that your spouse may not want your advice.

DON CHILDERS,
MARRIAGE AND FAMILY
COUNSELOR, AS QUOTED
IN *WHAT NO ONE
TELLS THE BRIDE*

it makes to do this my way, she will *want* to change!" How surprised and amazed we are to find that, despite our best examples, our spouse is perfectly satisfied to continue on in the same way. The more you try to hint or cajole or push or subtly criticize, the more that other person digs in. You can change yourself, and your spouse can change herself. But neither of you can change the other. Understand it, accept it, and get over it.

A caveat of marriage is that you are not going to change your spouse. Let that go.

5. *Learn to apologize.* Learning to apologize has been hard for both of us. Admitting we're wrong is threatening and frightening, and it makes us feel vulnerable. Learning to apologize has meant learning to really trust each other not to take advantage of one another in the weakened state of admitting to being wrong. Remember the old movie line from the sixties, "Love means never having to say you're sorry"? We would like to rewrite that to say, "Love means being *safe enough* to say you're sorry." Yes, it hurts to apologize. And yes, it is humbling to admit you were wrong. But look at the positive side: apologizing is freeing. It is cleansing. And it clears the way for the loving, open exchange that can move your marriage from "okay" to "great."

6. *Learn to accept apologies.* It's especially hard to apologize to someone who doesn't know how to accept an apology in a graceful manner. How do you respond to an apology? With a reproachful look? A self-satisfied air that insists "it's about time you admitted you were wrong"? Or does your body language speak loving forgiveness—the squeeze of a hand, a hug, a smile? Apologies have given us opportunities for some of our most tender moments. It draws us together in respect and causes us to genuinely desire to listen to one another more carefully. We are relieved and grateful that the conflicting tension has broken. And when one of us breaks that barrier and says, "I'm sorry," the other person is more willing to apologize another time. It pays to listen to an apology with an open heart!

7. Just do it. Sometimes the best way to deal with an irritation is to just forget about it. You may think if you let it slide, it will become a habit. Then you'll be stuck with forever picking up the socks (or recapping the toothpaste, writing the balance in the checkbook, putting the lid on the butter, making the bed) for the rest of your natural life. Maybe. Then again, maybe not. Perhaps if you stop lecturing and snapping and otherwise reacting, your partner just might go ahead and surprise you by doing it. Or maybe the problem is it just isn't important to your partner, so all the nagging in the world isn't going make a positive change anyway. At the very least, your home with the uncapped toothpaste or unmade bed will be a more peaceful place.

The tongue must be heavy indeed, because so few people can hold it.

QUESTION:
How do you respond when your partner apologizes?

When you make a conscious decision, you are able to willingly release the thing that is causing you the stress and let it go. The question, then, becomes one of making choices between what to hold on to and what to decide to let go. (Most people, we might say—including both of us!—err on the side of stressing over way too many little things.)

SMALL, SMALLER, SMALLEST

So, which of the irritating small stuff is big enough to sweat? We have a friend who wears a kilt to every event that even approaches formality. Big enough? No. One woman we know carries everything in her purse from a hammer to a shower cap to a pair of fold-up binoculars to a spool of thread with no needle in her purse. Big enough? Nah.

Kay's first husband used to carry three Swiss Army knives and alternate which one he cut his fingernails with. Big enough? Huh-uh. Kay herself won't drink coffee or even try anything that smacks of a coffee taste. Big enough? Nope. Dan insists on shining his shoes even when we're late. Big enough? Not even close.

Here's another in our long list of positive things about getting married later in life: It is more likely that we over-thirty-fives have learned the truth that if our spouses have a few quirks and hang-ups, so what? Ignore them. Better yet, accommodate them. Best of all, celebrate them. They are what make people unique and interesting. Besides, the more we are aware of our partner's quirks, the more toler-ant he or she is likely to be of ours. And won't that make for a happier home?

Answering our survey, Clifford wrote, "Anything that is really important to Paula is fine with me, and she feels the same about what I think I need to do."

Really? Take a peek at what Paula wrote—completely sep-arate from Clifford, by the way: "If something is extremely important to Clifford, I feel it is not a problem. If something is very, very important to me, Clifford says, no problem. All the rest is little stuff and I am in charge of little stuff."

Now, there's a couple that is in the process of weaving one beautiful piece of cloth!

"With age, I've learned patience, tolerance and listen-ing," John observed.

Here's a good rule: If you have to ask if something is big enough to sweat, it probably isn't. Ask yourself, "On a scale of one to ten, is this an eight or above?" If the answer is no, look the other way and move on.

If we have people over for dinner, who is responsible for cooking, cleaning, setting the table, creating the right atmosphere? This has been a constant area of conflict and is directly related to having developed our own styles of entertaining during our years of being single.

LYNN

Your action won't be lost on your spouse. And you will likely find that your partner will return the favor by cutting you some slack, too. The result will be a more enjoyable, stress-free day-by-day relationship.

Clifford wisely advises, "Develop a sense of humor and laugh at the things that happen."

Your marriage will be the winner.

Write down one small thing you will vow to stop sweating from this day forward.

FOR DISCUSSION

Replace the small stuff you are no longer going to sweat with small acts of love you are going to insert into your life. You may or may not want to keep the suggestions we start off with. Either way, make the list uniquely your own.

1. Relearn walking (discover the joy of a twilight walk together).

2. Tell each other about your dreams (both real and visionary).

3. Buy each other copies of your favorite books.

4. _____

5. _____

6. _____

7. _____

8. _____

9. _____

10. _____

11. _____

12. _____

13. _____

14. _____

15. _____

Fight Right

When Janet and I have a disagreement, we start out with a lot of yelling," Peter, the Irish Bostonian, told us. "After a while, when we calm down a bit, we are finally able to talk about the issue."

Another couple reported, "Dave hates fighting. He never raises his voice. He doesn't like conflict and he avoids it any way he can."

Good for Dave and shame on Janet and Peter, right? Doesn't happily-ever-after mean no quarreling or arguing?

Wrong. Disagreements and disputes are a fact of real life. Diane Sollee, director of the Coalition for Marriage, Family and Couples Education, says: "We need to get the message out and tell people before they get married that it's OK to fight. Right now we're sending people out onto the football field and not telling them the rules."

The question is not whether you will have conflicts. The question is, will those conflicts strengthen your marriage or will they damage it? Wouldn't it be wonderful to be able to discuss your differences in ways that actually strengthened your union and improved your intimacy?

Maureen's eyes narrow skeptically at such a suggestion. "I cannot compromise what I feel for the sake of another per-

> *I've been surprised at how much we disagree, given that I thought we were a lot alike and had many similar convictions about the world.*
>
> ANTHONY

son," she insists. "I may soften the edges a bit, but I cannot compromise my values or belief system. Neither of us likes to argue, but I probably will bring up a topic before James will as I am a fairly brave person in this regard. We've had some bad arguments, and they don't leave me feeling very good."

Yet here Maureen's skepticism starts to wane. "But, weathering those kinds of storms, I believe, has made us stronger. We are learning we can argue and neither one is leaving. That is always a fear I have, but I feel I have to take this risk to have a real and authentic life, with its ups and downs, good times and bad times. I have had to learn how to soften up a bit, to be patient and definitely to learn that being right sometimes just isn't as important as being cherished."

It really *isn't* impossible to strengthen your marriage through your conflicts. It's not even unrealistic.

Successful couples don't let their disagreements poison the rest of their relationship. They don't stop speaking to each other. They don't play mean tricks on each other. They don't try to injure each other. They don't nurse their hurts and allow the disagreements to fester into love-destroying patterns of behavior. Successful couples fight, but they fight right.

Know the Difference Between Reacting and Responding

In times of conflict, when we are angry and feel threatened, we automatically *react*. But if we are to protect our marriage, we need to resist that temptation and choose a better route. Instead of *reacting*, we need to *respond*. What is the difference, you ask? Plenty. Take a look at some examples:

Reacting says: "So, it's all *my* fault, huh? You blame everything on me!"

Responding says: "Let's work this out together."

The number one predictor of divorce is the habitual avoidance of conflict.

Diane Sollee, Founder and Director, Coalition for Marriage, Family and Couples Education

Many argue; not many converse.

Louisa May Alcott

Reacting says: "Yeah? Well, you're not so perfect yourself! I've got a few gripes I've been wanting to tell you and now is as good a time as any!"

Responding says: "We both make plenty of mistakes, but let's agree to deal with just this one issue now."

I've learned the importance of being patient—something that doesn't come naturally to me—and of choosing my words carefully.

MAUREEN

Reacting says: "You make me so mad! You are always so stubborn and hardheaded. You never listen to anything I say!"

Responding says: "It's hard for us to talk when we're angry. Let's give it a rest and come back in an hour when we've had time to cool down."

Reacting says: "See? See? Your socks are on the floor again! I knew it! It's the same thing, day after day, week after week. You'll never, ever change!"

Reponding says: "I moved the hamper next to your closet door so it would be more convenient for you to put your dirty socks in."

- *Reacting* causes further problems; *responding* solves problems.

- *Reacting* escalates an argument; *responding* attempts to defuse it.

- *Reacting* stirs up anger; *responding* creates a bridge between the two of you.

- *Reacting* locks you into dealing with the same issues over and over; *responding* lets you move on.

- *Reacting* makes you say really stupid things; *responding* allows you to back off and cool down.

- *Reacting* causes you to jump into a situation without considering the consequences; *responding* lets you step back and consider your options.

- *Reacting* says, "You are a stupid idiot, and I was a fool for ever marrying you! Everyone said I could have done better, and they were right, but I wouldn't listen, and now here I am stuck in this dump with you!" *Responding* says, "We are too angry to think rationally. Let's stop now before we say something we're sorry for later."

Before Mark and Rebecca married, both were in charge of their families and both were the boss at work. Once they married, you can imagine what their home was like. Reacting was a way of life! But Mark and Rebecca didn't like what they were seeing, and so they purposely set out to make changes. "We had to learn it was okay for us to be different and to accept each other's differences," Rebecca said. "It was not the end of the world if we didn't agree on everything. "

Reacting is a choice.

Responding is a much better choice.

QUESTION:
Are you a "reactor" or a "responder"? Where could you choose to make a change?

SO WHAT ARE THE RULES?

Look in any book on marriage, talk to any marriage counselor, and you will get a list of rules for handling conflict. And, yes, we've got a list for you too. We call ours the Eight Great Fight Fizzlers.

1. Set a timer.

2. Post your "Don't-Go-Theres."

3. Outlaw threats and ultimatums.

4. Fight fair.

5. Avoid pushing each other's hot buttons.

6. Don't fight when you are tired or stressed.

7. Learn what works best at calming the situation.

8. Accept that there are areas where you need to agree to disagree.

Fight Fizzler # 1: Set a Timer

Don't let the fight go on and on and on. For us, this is an important rule. It bothers Dan immensely that Kay says the same thing again and again. He takes it as endless nagging and harping. He feels that the issue itself could be dealt with in five or ten minutes—exceeding that seems to him like an attempt to "win" rather than explain.

For Kay, it is a desperate attempt to be certain she is heard—not wise, mind you, but desperate. A timer lets each person know they have only so much time to speak and only so much time to listen. It forces each person to be concise and then to let it go. And because a point is only going to be made once, the other partner is more likely to pay attention. The end result is that Kay makes her point only once and Dan is more likely to acknowledge he heard it.

Fight Fizzler #2: Post Your "Don't-Go-Theres"

Don't-go-theres are the things you want to avoid saying or doing because they will always, without exception, pour gasoline on the situation and turn it into a roaring inferno. Some examples that respondents to our survey offered were:

- "No wonder your 'ex' turned to alcohol!"

- "That sounds exactly like something your crazy father would say."

- "Are you going to get suicidal again?"

- "Being adopted, who knows what's in your background?"

Dissension in a house will lead to its destruction.

TALMUD

Sit down when you are both rested and in a good mood, and make a list of your "don't-go-theres." Then post that list somewhere such as on the closet door. Go over it until it is so seared into your brain that you would no sooner insert one of those zingers into an argument than stick your hand in a gas-fed fire.

Fight Fizzler #3: Outlaw Threats and Ultimatums
"All right then, maybe I will just pack my things and leave."

Many times, at the most basic level, an argument is about supporting each other even when you disagree. Once a partner introduces the idea of abandonment into the relationship, a seed of distrust has been planted. And once it is planted, it can easily begin to grow.

Get it into your mind when you are calm and sane that once those words leave your mouth, they can never be taken back. The seed, once planted, cannot be uprooted. Ultimatums and threats can be deadly to a relationship.

"Like all couples, we disagree," said Maureen, "but we never let our disagreements become bigger or stronger than us. Our creed is that divorce isn't an option. For me, this is really important because I waited thirty-seven years to meet James and I'll never be willing to let him go—unless we've explored all other alternatives, and I know there will always be at least one more to consider."

Fight Fizzler #4: Fight Fair
Here is where the rules come in.

- Drop comparisons—to Mama or Dad, or sister or brother, or anyone else—but especially to that "other spouse."

- No name calling.

QUESTION:
Have any angry threats or ultimatums escaped your lips? What can you do to express your heartfelt remorse to your spouse? Are you willing to ask God to keep your lips sealed against threats or ultimatums in the future?

- No sarcasm, insults or exaggeration.

- Stick to the problem at hand without dredging up past troubles.

- Allow your spouse to talk without interruption. Force yourself to listen to the other side. You just might learn something!

Really, when you think about it, all these rules can be encapsulated into what we know as the Golden Rule: *Do unto others as you would have them do unto you.*

Fight Fizzler #5: Avoid Pushing Each Other's Hot Buttons

The more we get to know each other, the closer we are, the more we confide in each other, the more vulnerable we become. That's because we know each other's tender spots. We also know what is sure to set each other off. Those are the very things to avoid.

"Russell hates it when I compare him to someone else," Sophie told us. "If I say, 'Look at how hard he works,' or 'He always does such nice things for his wife,' Russell says, 'Don't compare me!' To me, I'm not being critical, but I am careful not to do it because I know Russell hates it."

Fight Fizzler #6: Don't Fight When You Are Tired or Stressed

"Small disagreements are worsened when fatigue is a factor," Mark observed, "especially if both of you are tired. With me almost fifty-five and Rebecca forty-seven, we are usually good at recognizing this. If one gets cranky or tense, that person usually points out that it's not a good time to talk about a problem and asks to come back to it later. The other understands the wisdom and agrees."

Difficult to do? Absolutely. But an important goal to aim for.

Fight Fizzler #7: Learn What Works Best at
Calming the Situation

Knowing that conflict will happen, it is important to be ready with tactics for calming the situation. Granted, it's difficult when tempers are flaring, but it certainly helps to have thought it out ahead of time.

- Don't counterattack.

- Keep your unsolicited advice to yourself.

- Take turns restating what *you* see as the issue you're fighting about.

- Listen to what your spouse is saying without judging.

- Let him or her know you hear.

- Give up the right to be right all the time.

- Entertain the shattering possibility that the argument could be your fault.

- Very often, an argument grows up out of an unmet need. Identify that need and there is no reason to argue.

- Take your eyes off the specifics and focus instead on the heart of what is being said. That will allow you to stop quibbling about the details ("Oh yeah? Well, for your information, I did too once wash the dishes without being told. It was after we got home from the party at the Spencers'...").

- Don't jump on your spouse for his or her feelings even if you don't share them. ("It's stupid to be hurt about something like that!")

One wife, understanding that her husband is extremely nonconfrontational, has learned how to calm situations that arise between them. When she gets angry, he will listen to what she has to say. When she has said her piece, they go to separate rooms for an hour or so, then they come back to the table, listen to each other's point of view, and come to a mutual conclusion. Neither raises their voice. "He saw enough fighting in his childhood and his first marriage," she says.

He doesn't even refer to these as disagreements. He calls them "realignment ways of thinking."

Fight Fizzler #8: Accept That There Are Areas Where You Need to Agree to Disagree

Not every conflict can be resolved. Dr. John Gottman's research indicates that even in happy marriages, most fights are about "perpetual problems." We certainly saw this reflected in our surveys.

Scott wrote, "I think our biggest disagreements have been about my job, its demands and the interpersonal dynamics of the family business. I think I have made adjustments, but Andrea has revised her expectations too. The actual process has been one of discussion, compromise and, where that isn't possible, agreeing to disagree."

Couples worry that if they were better people, or better at being a wife or husband, they wouldn't have issues. That just isn't so. Some issues simply cannot be solved. Marital peace comes from understanding and accepting this.

"We used to have a very difficult time settling disagreements, until we read *Men Are from Mars, Women Are from Venus*," Nancy told us. "Truthfully, that saved many an argument from escalating out of hand. We keep our sense of humor now. I still read the daily readings every morning to remind me of how different we are. Jeff just thinks of things like sex and money and work much differently than I do. I have to constantly remind myself that we do not think alike and it's okay to be different."

"Peter and I do have disagreements, but the underlying rock of stability is the Lord and our commitment to being married," said Janet. "We've had some very difficult years, and we just persevered through them, asking forgiveness and moving forward. There have been times when we just couldn't agree. If it was a really important decision, like moving to a new house, then after much prayer I gave it up to the Lord and submitted to my husband's decision. That was very difficult, but it turned out to be okay."

Still, Sophie admits to getting frustrated when Russell doesn't see things her way. In all honesty, she wants him to agree with her. Yet she states, "I'm learning that it's okay to disagree as long as at heart we truly respect each other."

It helps to create a sort of buffer zone of space until tempers cool to the point where an issue can be discussed in a calmer setting
SCOTT

KEYS TO RESOLUTION

In our opinion, technology has been a boon to conflict resolution, especially in a two-computer family like ours.

E-Mail

E-mail can be a nice way to argue. You can write out what you want to say, then sit back, read it and think, *Hmmm . . . I don't think that's exactly what I want to say after all . . .* and you can do some editing. You might read it again and think, *I know I'm angry, but that sounds a bit too harsh . . .* and you can make more changes. After it's written, it's a good idea to set it aside while you let yourself cool down, then read it again and, if need be, make more changes. In the end, you pass along something much nicer and kinder and gentler than you would have if you had just blurted out what was on your mind when you were angry.

There's a benefit for the recipient, too. That person can

I'm not sure we are the type who ever "settle" anything. We talk, we fight, we discuss; sometimes we reach agreement on a particular issue. We often come back at it again from another perspective at a later date.

LYNN

QUESTION:
Think back to a recent disagreement or quarrel (without getting into it again, of course). What things did each of you do to bring it to an end?

read it and digest it at his or her leisure, then take time in responding. Because that person isn't torn between listening and forming a response, he or she can focus all attention on what is written down. Just the message—no tone of voice or body language to read.

When this idea came up in our ten-couple roundtable discussion, Rebecca was especially excited. "Mark and I are both really passionate people," she said. "When we feel something, we feel it very deeply. That can cause problems. One thing we are learning together—partly because we are older—is that we can identify that in ourselves. I've even told Mark at times, 'I'm feeling "major-emotional" right now talking about this. We need to wait. I can't do this right now.' And Mark's done the same. E-mailing each other would help us."

Wait Time

Another resolution key is wait time. Many couples stated that they moved apart for a specific amount of time to allow each of them to cool down before they resolved the conflict. The key here is to set a specific time to come back together. To simply say, "We'll work it out later," and then let it hang unresolved, is most unsatisfying and can lead to real resentment.

Wait time should be no more than twenty-four hours, preferably less than that. A good way to set it is to say, "I'm too upset to talk right now. Let's meet at the kitchen table in two hours."

See Two Sides

Why is it so hard to take the blame and say, "I was wrong"? No, not because you are both stubborn and mule-headed. Think about it: we see a conflict only from our own perspective. If we could look at it calmly and rationally from our partner's perspective, it might appear entirely different.

The fact is, however you slice it, that issue you are haggling over has two sides. And you can never see both of them until you close your mouth and listen to the other person. It is vital that you come to where you can see it from your spouse's point of view.

Apologize and Accept the Other's Apology

Not everyone is able to fit in with the same apologize-and-forgive pattern. Do you want to do your relationship a favor? Expand your definition of *apology*. Saying the words "I'm sorry" doesn't have to be the only way to adequately apologize. A hug and a kiss will also work quite well. Or how about a hug with an admission of: "I should have listened to you. Next time I will." Or how about a dozen red roses? Or maybe your favorite home-cooked dinner and your hand squeezed during grace.

Whatever it is, accept it gracefully as the apology it is meant to be. It is impossible to put a value on grace extended from one spouse to another.

"It is very hard for me to sit on my anger and think before I speak," Sophie admits. "Yet when I react quickly, eight times out of ten, after I calm down, I'm sorry . . . *really* sorry . . . for what I said. One thing I really appreciate about Russell is that he never holds it against me. And he could, because I've said some very, very hurtful things. But he doesn't. He just lets it go."

Sophie mused, "If I had married when I was younger, I think my marriage would have had much conflict. My friends tell me I have changed a lot over the years, through God's grace and healing—that I have become less tense, less intimidated and more content with life. My family says that since I've been married, I've changed even more—when you

Anthony is much better at saying he is sorry than I am. I do it with difficulty and not very graciously.

LYNN

The power to forgive lies not in the person who has hurt us, but in ourselves.

DR. PAUL COLEMAN,
THE FORGIVING
MARRIAGE

are loved and accepted for who you are, it can be very healing. Because I know how deeply Russ loves me, I find it very
difficult to say 'no' to him when he asks me do something
that is important to him."

THE INTIMACY OF KINDNESS

Want to know a secret that is almost guaranteed to keep
your arguments from escalating into fights? Here it is: *treat
each other kindly.* Yes, that's it, that's all there is to it.
Doesn't sound all that profound, you say? Maybe not, but
you'd be surprised at how effective it is. Studies have shown
that happy, stable couples treat each other with kindness
and respect. In short, they are nice to each other.

The problem is, it is awfully easy for couples to fall into a
pattern of subtle unkindness toward each other. Let us show
you what we mean: Being as honest as you can, give yourself
a little kindness test. (*Yourself.* No fair nudging your spouse
while you do this.)

- Do you speak with an irritable edge to your voice?

- Do you give orders instead of requests?

- Do you lecture?

- Do you talk to others about your spouse's irritating
  traits when your spouse is sitting right there listening?

- Do you speak for your partner instead of letting your
  partner speak for him or herself?

- Do you make belittling comments—even in jest?

- Do you contradict your spouse in public?

If you answered *yes* to even one of the questions, you have
some remedial kindness work to do. If you had more than one
yes, well . . . let's just say you had better get started now!

You say you think you're just fine in this area? No improvement needed? Maybe. But before you skip on to the next chapter, take one more step: check with your spouse. He or she may see it differently. You just might be surprised at the answer you'll get. And if the answers do catch you off guard—that is, you're not as "just fine" in an area as you thought—don't be defensive about it. Go back and review the "Keys to Resolution" that begin on page 163. The point is to help resolve an issue that bothers your partner, not to create another thing to fight about!

Being respectful and kind can go a long, long way toward forging a relationship that deepens and deepens through the years, for as long as you two shall live. Andrea and Scott are well on their way. "One of the things I most love about Scott is that 98 percent of the time (which is far more than most people) he gives high priority to my needs and wishes," Andrea said. "He calls me his 'princess,' and that sort of says it all. He wouldn't be human without the other two percent! I try to do the same for him, but I confess that he is much better at it than I am."

BOTTOM LINE

We have discussed a number of techniques for handling conflicts. These techniques only help, however, if you know what it is you are fighting about. Often the real conflict isn't the socks left piled on the floor or the empty milk carton in the refrigerator or the check that wasn't recorded in the checkbook. Those are just irritants. The real conflict isn't even the bigger issue of who has to do the most work around the house or how you spend your money. It is the deep-down issues—maybe even subconscious issues—of your spouse's seeming lack of respect for you or his or her lack of concern for your feelings.

Love your spouse abundantly. Speak your love often. Let love shine in your eyes and be seen in your every action.

There are times when it can be very helpful (and extremely wise) to have a third party assist you. A counselor can provide a safe forum and a degree of guidance that will keep you from getting too frightened and falling into the dirty fighting that can cause lingering wounds and deep resentment.

"Counseling may not be essential," John observed, "but it certainly can be helpful."

I avoid acknowledging guilt because I don't believe I deserve to be forgiven.

LYNN

Certainly, counseling is no quick or easy miracle cure, because you are dealing with issues of personality, heredity and upbringing. But it can give you insight into those issues, help you see why you do what you do, and give you some tools to deal with the issues that are causing you trouble.

For instance, through a counselor's help we came to realize we both have a deep need to be appreciated. People with our type of personality profile often have a deep-seated drive to do things for others—not for material gain or favors but for the sake of altruism, plus a little "thank you," or at least some recognition. That is why, without being asked and without ulterior motives (other than appreciation), we both truly enjoy doing things for one another.

And so long as we both feel appreciated most of the time, all is well. But inevitably, "stuff" sometimes gets in the way of our acknowledging the other's efforts. It's unintentional and almost always due to distractions and "busyness," but not stinginess or tit-for-tat. Regardless, when it happens, pretty soon the ignored one is feeling taken for granted. That in turn leads to withdrawal, where we say very little to one another—sometimes for days—or even to arguing about all the wrong issues ("You don't care about anything good I do, you just point out all my faults!" "Well, you don't love me! You just take without ever giving back!") and getting further and further away from the basic problem.

Our counselor helped us cut through all the flak and see the basic problem—the need for appreciation. Going without it is, for us, like trying to go without air or food or water.

Once we realized this, the solution was fairly simple: give one another the appreciation and recognition we both crave. But just because it's simple doesn't mean it's easy. What gets in the way is that some sort of apology is usually a necessary first step, and as we've already said, apologies don't roll right off our tongues. For another thing, we both have a tendency to hang onto the hurt of the original oversight and not accept appreciation after the fact very well.

These may be childish traits. Although they're embarrassing to admit, we are glad to say that little by little we are being weaned off them. What has really helped is the way our counselor, a devout Christian, works with us. She begins and ends our sessions in prayer. When we humble ourselves before God and ask his forgiveness, we cannot help but wonder, "How can I ask him for what I am unwilling to give another, especially one so dear to me?" That makes it much easier for us to give up our own hurts and submit to one another.

Whether they've had professional help or not, couples who fight fair pick up on the underlying hidden agenda. They hear what is unspoken, and they respond by letting their partners know how much they are respected and cared about and loved. That's why fighting right can actually strengthen your marriage. It allows you to air your differences and to make connections in places that are shaky between you. It helps you to see each other's places of weakness and vulnerability, and to find compromises with which you can both live.

On the door of our bedroom closet we have this verse prominently posted: "A gentle answer turns away wrath, but a harsh word stirs up anger" (Proverbs 15:1).

Sometimes we get so caught up in working on the difficulties in our relationship that we forget to stop and celebrate the joys.

KAY AND DAN

It really is true, you know. We have tried it and proved it. To encourage you to do the same, here are some soft words you might want to try (and an idea of the wrath they will help to turn away!):

If You Say	You Will Turn Away
Your feelings are important to me.	*All you think of is yourself!*
What can we do to make this better?	*How can I win this fight?*
I'm sorry I hurt you.	*I'll get back at you!*
Tell me your side.	*You always think you're right!*
I love you.	*You don't care about me.*

Refresh your spirit and your love with time together in a quiet, special place. Put aside your troubles for the moment and speak only of the love you share.

"Fights? Never! Only local skirmishes!" John says of his life with Lillian. And he has no problem knowing whom to thank. "It always goes back to the Lord and his love for us. If we are not responding to him and his love, nothing beyond that is going to work. The Lord is the secret, and it is no secret that we cast ourselves upon him."

Mark echoes what John has to say. "I would be much more difficult to live with if not for the Lord. The last time I got very angry was on vacation in Hawaii last summer. I thought Rebecca and our daughters had thoughtlessly dumped me in Lahaina and were so preoccupied with shopping they didn't care if I found them or not. They weren't at the prearranged meeting spot and I searched up and down the street for half an hour in the hot afternoon sun. When I finally connected they were oblivious, which made me even angrier, so I mumbled angry words under my breath at Rebecca. As we walked to the car she kept saying things like, 'What *is* your problem?' Back at the condo I retreated into the bedroom and prayer.

"Eventually even I was shocked by how disproportionate

my anger was to the situation. I still felt Rebecca and the girls were inconsiderate, especially Rebecca as the adult and group leader, but God convicted and motivated me to take responsibility for my part. I figure, *Men are called to be leaders of the house. If you want your wife to be more loving and understanding, then lead the way and you be more loving and understanding.* We are called to lead by example. I would always fall back on blame and selfishness if not for the Lord."

Praying together helps to resolve conflict. It may feel forced at first, but give God a chance to soften your hearts.

FOR DISCUSSION

- Are there recurring themes to your conflicts?

- Are you able to handle these in a good-natured way? ("Yeah, yeah, don't even tell me—you forgot to pick up the cleaning again. Too bad—the pie shop coupon clipped to the receipt expired today.") Or does it invariably turn into full-blown war?

- Go back to the "Keys to Resolution" earlier in this chapter and talk specifically about how you might calm these recurring conflicts.

Living Life God's Way

We were at a Christian couples' conference at Mount Hermon, California, and the speaker was just winding up. It had been raining all weekend, and the sun had finally broken through the gloom. A gentle breeze rustling through the redwoods scattered the remaining clouds. We were itching to get outside. That's when the speaker picked up his Bible and read Micah 6:8: "What does the LORD require of you? To act justly and to love mercy and to walk humbly with your God."

Dan looked at Kay, then took her hand in his and squeezed it. Kay snuggled over a little closer, and the sunshine and redwoods were forgotten. Something far more beautiful had just happened.

That's because Dan knows how very special those words are to Kay. He knows that although Kay was raised in a Christian home and went to a Christian school, her faith didn't mean a great deal to her personally. He also knows what a turning point in her faith the year she turned thirteen was. He knows because Kay told him.

This is what she said: "That year I decided to read through the entire Bible—partly because I wanted to impress people, but mostly because I wanted to impress God. A lot of it was boring and hard to get through, but I kept at it. And then in August I got to Micah 6. Oh, Dan, when I read those verses my eyes filled with tears! All the long list of rules I had been taught! All the punishments that had terrified me as long as I could remember! And all the time God's true requirements were right in his Word. That day, I read and reread those three verses so many times that I memorized them. And though I've recited them a hundred times since, I can never get through that beautiful passage without tears filling my eyes. That's when I first experienced God."

Dan knows Kay's story because he listened when she told it to him. And Kay knows Dan's story because she was there when it happened.

Dan's story occurred several years before we were married. Although he didn't really understand what it meant to be a believer in Jesus Christ, on occasion he had attended church with Kay and her husband Larry before Larry's illness made it impossible for him to go. Now Kay was attending a small Bible study of committed believers who were starting a new church plant, and Dan repeatedly asked if he might attend. Finally Kay reluctantly brought him along. Very quickly it became apparent that Dan was not "one of the group." (When it was time for prayer, he asked, "Do we need to know the words, or do we just talk off the top of our heads like Kay and Larry do before they eat?")

As soon as the prayer time was over, Randy and Mark—two of the four men in the group—came up to Dan and said, "It was so nice to have you here! How about joining us for a Bible study tomorrow?" The next morning they met at six-thirty. Dan had no study Bible, and the only extra one Kay had to lend him was her Women's Devotional Bible with a pink, flowery cover. Once given a taste of what he had always hungered for without knowing it, Dan proved to be a

With what shall I come before the LORD and bow down before the exalted God? Shall I come before him with burnt offerings, with calves a year old? Will the LORD be pleased with thousands of rams, with ten thousand rivers of oil? Shall I offer my firstborn for my transgression, the fruit of my body for the sin of my soul? He has showed you, O man, what is good. And what does the LORD require of you? To act justly and to love mercy and to walk humbly with your God.

MICAH 6:6-8

voracious Bible student. He ended up becoming the first new believer at Christ Presbyterian Church, and that Bible study of three grew into the church's first men's Bible study.

We love our how-we-got-here-in-the-Lord stories!

It is a wonderful thing for couples to be dearest friends. But just imagine the unique place that friendship must hold when you carry it on into the spiritual realm. To be dearest *spiritual* friends—now that is a worthy goal indeed!

Some couples start out further along the road toward spiritual friendship than others. Even before they were married, Paula and Cliff had already shared much of their mutual spiritual journeys with each other. For two years, they had attended the same Bible study and they prepared for it together. "Doing those lessons together showed us a lot about where the other stood on spiritual issues," Cliff said.

Lillian and John also had a spiritual history. For over ten years Lillian and her first husband had contributed to John and his first wife's mission work in Guatemala. Whenever the missionary couple was in Missouri, they stayed with Lillian and her family. The four of them talked and shared deeply about their spiritual selves.

Other couples, however, struggle to take their very first steps. "Russell isn't one to be open about his feelings," Sophie told us. "To be perfectly honest, I'm not sure where he is spiritually." Then she added a bit wistfully, "I wish I did know."

We called Sophie and asked her a simple question: "Have you ever asked him?" She hadn't. Then we asked, "Have you ever told him about a time you really felt God's love in your life?" She said no, that the subject had never come up.

SHARING YOUR SPIRITUAL SELF

On a rainy November evening the subject finally "came up." Sophie recalls it clearly.

He [Jesus] works on us in all sorts of ways: But above all, He works on us through each other.

C. S. LEWIS, MERE CHRISTIANITY

A fire crackled in the fireplace and she sat close to Russell on the couch, sharing a bowl of popcorn. "Did I ever tell you I went to Haiti with a group of teen-agers from my church?" she asked.

"You? To Haiti? I can't believe it!" Russ exclaimed. "What did you do there?"

"Helped build an orphanage. And taught Bible school every day for two weeks. You know, that was the first time I remember really seeing God at work . . . "

Sophie ended up talking for over an hour, with Russell interrupting now and then to ask questions and make comments. At the end, Russell stared in perplexed wonder as tears ran down the cheeks of his staunchly unemotional wife as she told him, "I decided there in Haiti that I wanted to be a missionary. There is no higher calling."

"And yet you're an artist and a business person. So what happened?"

"When I got home, everyone laughed and teased me. They said I wouldn't last for two weeks on the mission field. I guess they convinced me. After a while I put the idea out of my mind. And yet, sometimes I can't help wondering . . . Russ, do *you* think I could have made it as a missionary?"

Russ put his arms around Sophie and hugged her tightly. "I *know* you could have."

For a while, Sophie tells us, they sat watching the fire in silence. Then Sophie asked, "Did you ever have an experience when you really felt God's love? I mean, personally?"

For several minutes, Russ didn't answer. Finally he said, "I thought I did once, but then God let me down." And for the first time he told Sophie the story of his firstborn child— a son born two months prematurely who lived less than a week. "I prayed and prayed for my son's life, and God didn't answer me. I had trusted God, and then when I needed him most, he let me down."

Where two or three come together in my name, there am I with them.

JESUS, IN
MATTHEW 18:20

After almost eight years of marriage, Russ and Sophie shared their spiritual selves with each other for the very first time. Paula and Cliff, and Lillian and John, would find that very difficult to comprehend. Maybe you do, too. Or maybe you understand it perfectly well. Some people just do find it hard to discuss their spiritual selves with their spouses. What if that person who means more to you than anyone else in the world doesn't want to hear what you have to say? Or laughs at you? Or criticizes or judges you? Or maybe trivializes what is so precious and dear to you?

If you are one who struggles with sharing, you may find Sophie's approach helpful. Consider how she went about it. Like Sophie, perhaps you need to follow these steps.

Choose the time. Be careful not to try to have a meaningful conversation when there are other distractions (the television is on or the children are wanting attention), or when the other person is tired or in an off-mood, or when you are pushed for time.

Invite your spouse into the conversation. Rather than approaching it as a lecture, choose a casual approach where your spouse can gently opt out if it is not the right time for him or her.

Allow yourself to be vulnerable. Without vulnerability, there can be no spiritual intimacy. That is part of what makes it frightening to some people. And yet that willingness to be vulnerable before each other and together before God will bind the two of you together in a very special way. And very often—as was the case with Sophie and Russell—the vulnerability of one leads the other spouse to make him or herself vulnerable as well.

If it's hard to talk about the past, it's often even more difficult to talk about today. It's especially hard to share your spiritual struggles with your spouse.

"It's so much easier to go to a women's retreat and bare my soul," one woman said. "I can go home and never have to worry about seeing those ladies again—or at least not run into them every day. If I pour my heart out to my husband, every time I look at him, I'm faced with my own weaknesses again and again."

And then there is that unspoken fear: "What about when we get into an argument? Will he come at me with the ultimate weapon—that secret weakness I confided?"

Without a doubt, spiritual intimacy requires a strong foundation of trust. On the other hand, spiritual intimacy also *builds* a strong foundation of trust, so don't be deterred if you're not already there. Come at it in small steps. Rather than thinking of it as "pouring out your heart" or "baring your soul," think in terms of sharing one special moment or thought with the one who wants to know you best.

"I want my wife to know what is important to me, what I really feel strongly about," one young Texan told us. "But I just don't know how to express those things. I can talk about a lot of things, but that's not one of them. . . . And it doesn't help that I get the feeling that she isn't all that eager to hear what I have to say."

Again, it is important to ask for what you want. That husband might say, "Dear, could we go for a walk around the neighborhood after dinner tonight? Something has been running through my mind and I really want to share it with you. It will only take about ten or fifteen minutes." He should stick to his time limit—his wife might be resentful if he is still talking an hour later—and afterwards ask her for her thoughts.

THE COUPLE THAT PRAYS TOGETHER . . .

"Cliff and I pray together for fifteen minutes before we get out of bed in the morning," Paula told us. "We have done

- *Take turns telling each other about your first experience of knowing God's presence in your lives.*

- *Share a few details of your spiritual journeys.*

- *Tell about one person who was important in your spiritual life.*

- *What is one thing that especially encouraged you spiritually?*

that every day since the morning after our wedding."

First thing in the morning? When your hair is still sticking up and your breath would choke the dog and you're grumpy because you haven't had your coffee yet? *First* thing?

"It's a decision we made before we were married," Cliff agreed. "Prayer together would always be an integral part of our lives, and first thing in the morning is the only time that really works for us. In fact, if we aren't together in the morning—if I'm out of town on business or something—we both set our alarms ahead fifteen minutes so we can pray for each other before we get out of bed. Actually, it's a wonderful way to start the day."

There is nothing that says you have to pray together first thing in the morning. It's not the timing that matters; it's the prayer. And if we are honest, finding the time isn't the problem. It's that praying together isn't always easy. Unless you limit your couple prayer time to "God bless our family and the missionaries all around the world and be with us today and help Jimmy's cold to get well, Amen." But you are not going to get much out of that kind of all-purpose prayer, either.

The thing is, when you pray alone and silently, you can be totally honest with God. You can express your deepest hopes and fears. God won't laugh or mock you. He won't ever throw what you say back in your face. He won't think less of you once he hears you utter your tucked-away-in-the-back-corner terrors. He already knows about those secret sins and terrible joys you keep hidden away. But what if you were to pray all that out loud in front of your spouse? What then?

Like spiritual sharing, praying together requires a foundation of trusting friendship. It assumes a relationship where your prayers will truly be worship and thanksgiving to God, and requests on behalf of those who would further his kingdom. And certainly prayers for God's guidance in your fam-

Prayer together may not be so much a means to a good marriage as a result of it.

R. PAUL STEVENS,
MARRIAGE SPIRITUALITY

ily and for the affairs of your life together. What it would *not* be is veiled criticism of your spouse ("Dear Lord, help my husband to see the damage he is doing by persisting in . . ."). Or manipulation ("Father, my mother is coming to visit and I know it's hard on the family, but it might be her last year . . ."). Or threats ("Father God, you have set me as head over my wife, yet she refuses to obey as you have commanded. I commit her to you for punishment.")

Praying together was not easy for Peter and Janet. "I had this skeptical attitude," Peter admits. "I would rigorously question and challenge everything, and it really upset Janet. After a while we gave up trying to pray together, and that continued for years. Finally, about three years ago, we began to pray together every morning. It has drawn us closer to God and, surprisingly, to each other. We were stronger for it, which was a very good thing because we had some really tough times right around the corner."

Peter and Janet found that by adding a third strand to their marital cord, it became much stronger and more difficult to sever (see callout). There's a wonderful strengthening power to couples' prayer.

You don't need to start out baring your soul in prayer. Begin gently this way:

Pray silently together. Set aside a specific amount of time—say, ten minutes—and simply sit together as you each pray silently.

Keep a prayer book. In a notebook, list the people and events for which you want to thank God, verses you would like to read in praise and specific requests you want to present to the Lord. If you are nervous about what to say when you pray, write out the exact words and read them to the Lord.

Pray short, conversational prayers, one after the other, as if you were talking with a friend (which you are).

> *Though one may be overpowered, two can defend themselves. A cord of three strands is not quickly broken.*
>
> ECCLESIASTES 4:12

Pray in different ways. One of you may want to pray out loud, and the other only silently. Fine. Pray any way you can. As you get more comfortable, you will find the way that leads you both into greater spiritual intimacy.

SHARE GOD'S WORD

Early in our marriage, we (Dan and Kay) bought a chronological Bible. Beginning with "In the beginning, God . . ." in Genesis 1:1 and ending with "The grace of the Lord Jesus be with God's people. Amen" in Revelation 22:21, it helps readers see the Bible unfold in chronological order. That's the Bible from which we read aloud. It's taking us a long time to get through because we want to cross-reference everything in our other versions that have notes, but we are really enjoying it. Another couple told us they greatly appreciate the readings in one of the Bibles set up specifically for couples. They are reading through the Bible as we are doing, but they stop as they come to the devotions and exercises and spend time on them.

What a blessing it is to read God's Word together and then to talk about what you read!

"We've started reading the Bible together a hundred times, and we can never make it work," the mother of a blended family told us. "Believe me, I feel guilty about it, but the fact is, our entire life together we've had kids, and that just doesn't leave much regular couple-together time."

She's right. Some families are able to work out a plan for a family devotion at meal times. That's wonderful, and certainly a special family time, but it's not the couple time that we are talking about here. Some couples select a passage of scripture, each read it individually as they have time, then they discuss it at night before they go to bed.

"I find it difficult to share spiritually with my husband,"

another woman told us on the telephone, "and he really isn't interested in us praying together nor in reading the Bible. I was certain that spiritual intimacy was something that just wasn't to be for me. But friends of ours, who just happen to also attend our church, invited us to come to their home Bible study group, and it has made all the difference. Every Monday and Tuesday evening, my husband and I do our Bible study lessons together. It is the most wonderful time of the week for me!"

That is an excellent point. Our church puts a great emphasis on home study groups. Kay has led the Thursday evening women's Bible study for five years now, and Dan is a leader in the Wednesday evening men's Bible study at the Rescue Mission. Both are good and worthwhile and enjoyable, but we long to be together in a couple's group. We're determined to do it next year.

SPIRITUAL FULFILLMENT TOGETHER

Here's a story told by Kay: "In February, I came back from a mission trip to India and China where I had interviewed women for a book on Christians who live and serve in the hardest places on earth. I was so moved by what I saw and heard that I could hardly tell the stories without crying. Dan has heard my stories so many times he could easily tell every one of them. Yet somehow he remains distanced from those women I had come to love. He knows all the facts, but he doesn't know the people. He hasn't been there. So when I completed my interviews with a trip to North Africa and Egypt last month, Dan went along.

"This time Dan saw the suffering in the parched plains of Senegal where women walk hours just to get a few gallons of water. He listened as a woman in Morocco told us about two Christian women who starved to death because their Muslim families had disowned them and they were not allowed to work. In Tunisia, he ran with us to throw blankets over the Bibles and anything else that would mark us as Christians every time there was a knock on the door in the house where we stayed. In Egypt, he saw the crosses tattooed on the wrists of believers who, fearing they might not be able to stand up to persecution, wanted to be indelibly branded as Christians. When Dan tells about the believers in North Africa, he chokes with emotion. He not only knows the stories of those dear ones, he knows *them*. And what a difference it makes!"

Having married later, we both had already developed our own areas of ministry. We have our own areas of expertise and preference. But now there is a new wrinkle—we want to serve the Lord together, to support each other's ministries, to encourage the place where God has placed our partner.

Sometimes we don't like it very much.

Traveling to Africa and staying in some—shall we say— exceedingly rustic conditions is not what Dan feels called to do. On the other hand, getting up at first light and going to church to help set up the sound system is not what Kay feels to be her ministry. But we do want to be partners in what we do. Dan was able to participate in only part of what Kay did in Africa, but he became so close to the people that he made arrangements for a dear brother from Senegal to live with us for a month next spring! Kay has rearranged her Sunday morning schedule to accommodate Dan's need to be at church early in the morning.

Paul Stevens, in his excellent book *Marriage Spirituality: Ten Disciplines for Couples Who Love God*, writes: "I personally believe Christ would have us move not toward parity in ministry but full partnership. This is true not only for church leadership but also for simple ministries like leading a Bible study group as a couple. Parity communicates sameness and interchangeability; full partnership communicates that the differences can be appreciated and celebrated.[1]

FROM OUR HEARTS TO YOURS

There are lots and lots of decisions we have to make as couples, some a whole lot more important than others. We've covered many of them in this book, and we're sure you've thought of a few more. But of all of them, right here may be the most important one, for your spirituality forms the underpinning of who you truly are. As one savvy over-thirty-five couple to another, may we present you with a challenge? Talk together *right now* about what you might do to increase your spiritual intimacy. Then try it—*really try it*—for one week, and see if it doesn't make a difference in your relationship.

You say one week isn't a very long time? You're right. More time would be better. But we think even one week will convince you of the value of putting a high priority on developing this vital aspect of your relationship.

FOR DISCUSSION

Use this inventory to help you discover the state of your spiritual intimacy. Each partner is to answer for him or herself, *not for the other*. (Even though you may have a really, really good idea of how your partner should be marking the question, it is up to each of you to mark for yourself. You can go over it and discuss it later if you choose to.) Circle the number that best describes you under each statement, from 5 being Highly Agree and 1 being Strongly Disagree.

If my spouse and I could minister together anywhere, in any capacity, it would be:

(her answer)

_____

(his answer)

_____

[1]R. Paul Stevens, *Marriage Spirituality: Ten Disciplines for Couples Who Love God* (Downers Grove, Ill.: InterVarsity Press, 1989), p. 101.

Husband   **Wife**

I am open to sharing the stories of my spiritual journey.

5   4   3   2   1   1   2   3   4   5

I feel comfortable telling my spouse about my spiritual struggles and doubts.

5   4   3   2   1   1   2   3   4   5

I want the two of us to pray together daily.

5   4   3   2   1   1   2   3   4   5

It is of utmost importance that we read the Bible together on a regular basis.

5   4   3   2   1   1   2   3   4   5

We do have a spiritual ministry together.

5   4   3   2   1   1   2   3   4   5

We desire to find a spiritual ministry we can do together.

5   4   3   2   1   1   2   3   4   5

Now look over your scoring. Are there any areas in which both of you scored high? If so, congratulations! Take that strong foundation and build on it! If there are areas that are very low, see if you might come up with some baby steps to get you started in laying down the beginnings of a foundation in that area. For ideas, go back and reread the corresponding section in this chapter.

12

Love Never Fails

Not everyone marries by reciting the traditional wedding vows, but most everyone knows the most memorable phrases:

"For better or for worse."

"For richer or for poorer."

"In sickness and in health."

"Forsaking all others."

"Until death do us part."

These are powerful words. They signify commitment and fidelity no matter what may come. And "what" usually does come. A couple marrying in their thirties could very possibly live long enough to celebrate a fiftieth wedding anniversary or even beyond. Those who marry a decade or two later could still have thirty to forty years of married life. And during that much time, many things—both good and bad—can happen.

Even good things can create strains, and bad things certainly do. Getting along with and enjoying your spouse and your marriage is not all that hard when things are going well. It's when serious problems arise that the real commitment— the "for better or for worse"—is put to the test.

No couple intending to stay together for life should base that intention on the hope that nothing really serious will

As you grow to know your beloved, grow also to know the Lord who watches over you.

come along to upset their relationship. None of us can know when, where or even whether we will have to bear some unforeseen adversity.

Then why is it, when bad times come, that some couples unite in mutual support, care, forgiveness and encouragement to go on while others turn on each other or watch helplessly as their relationship falls apart? Is it purely a question of the quantity of their love? Or the quality?

WHAT ABOUT LOVE?

The apostle Paul, in 1 Corinthians 13—his great chapter on love—wrote:

> Love is patient, love is kind. It does not envy, it does not boast, it is not proud. It is not rude, it is not self-seeking, it is not easily angered, it keeps no record of wrongs. Love does not delight in evil but rejoices with the truth. It always protects, always trusts, always hopes, always perseveres. Love never fails.

So is that the secret? If somehow you are able to put all those wonderful attributes into practice toward your spouse and be a super-loving person, then is your marriage assured of surviving the tough times? Sorry! Remember, this is the ideal picture of love. It is the goal to which we aspire; the model set before us. But we are not perfect creatures. Try as we may, we will inevitably fall short of this ideal. No, you can't rely on achieving perfect love.

Not so with God. He can never *fail* to love perfectly, not only because he is perfect, but because he is love.

When hard times come, we can cling to our loving mate and hold on for dear life. In fact, we should. But that will bring no guarantees. It is when we cling together to our loving God for dear life, when we put our faith in him, living our belief in him every minute of every day, that we will

It is love in old age, no longer blind, that is true love. For love's highest intensity doesn't necessarily mean its highest quality. . . . Passersby commonly see little beauty in the embrace of young lovers on a park bench, but the understanding smile of an old wife to her husband is one of the loveliest things in the world.

BOOTH TARKINGTON, AUTHOR

make it through. It is the only way any of us can be assured of surviving in trying times—the only way a marriage can be certain to endure. We have been privileged to know numerous couples who provide excellent examples.

Not long ago, one of our middle-aged friends discovered he has a particularly nasty, virulent form of prostate cancer. Together, he and his wife are doing all they can to find a cure for it, or at least to prolong his well being as long as possible. But they are not well off, the treatments are expensive, time consuming and debilitating, and he isn't able to work like he used to. So his wife is now working three jobs to make ends meet. Is she bitter and complaining? No. They have always loved and served the Lord, and this tragedy has only brought them closer and made them both poignantly aware of just how much each means to the other. Their daily prayers together serve to deepen not only their love and devotion for one another, but for living God's word and doing his work in whatever way they still can.

God is love.

1 JOHN 4:8

We know of at least two other couples where the husband was severely incapacitated, in both cases by Chronic Fatigue Syndrome. Yet their wives, too, doubled their efforts both in providing for the families and caring for their ill husbands. Despite the extreme strain this long-lasting and insidious condition placed upon their marriages, both couples have endured. And both attribute that endurance not to their own abilities but to those attributes God gave them in answer to their prayers for help.

We also know of a number of couples with children who suffer afflictions, yet who have remained together, supporting one another through the pain and trials. In one family, two sons were born with profound mental deficiencies. Although in time both had to be institutionalized, their parents never wavered in their conviction that the Lord gave them those boys for his own good reasons. They found that in caring for their sons together, their love and respect for one another grew along with their ever-greater reliance on God for guidance and patience.

Other couples have endured great emotional pain and loss. Many of the couples we interviewed for this book were married before, some having their first marriages end through divorce and others through the death of a spouse. Yet they were willing to trust again, even to bear the pain of a beloved spouse's death again, because of a love in their hearts they wanted to share and, in many cases, their faith in the leading of the Lord.

John and Lillian were reluctant to marry for a reason they hated to admit even to themselves: they had both been caregivers for dying spouses, and they never wanted to have to go through that again.

"Quite honestly," Lillian said, "I didn't know if I would be up to it. I just couldn't bear the thought of watching John slip away from me the way my first husband did. But I didn't want to face the rest of my life without him by my side, either. We prayed a long time over what to do. Finally we came to feel the Lord had brought us together for a reason and that he would provide for us no matter what happened. That's when we decided to marry. Every day since, we have prayed for our continued good health and for our love for each other."

Paula had endured a bitter and soul-wrenching divorce. "I could not go through that again," she told us. "It was terrible, a living nightmare. Because of that awful specter, I shut myself off from any possibility of ever marrying again. But then I met Cliff and fell in love with him despite myself.

"Then one day I realized that he was nothing like my first husband, mainly because the Lord was the first thing in his life. Life with Cliff would be built around honoring God, something that was totally lacking in my first marriage. That was when I finally determined to trust God to heal my past wounds. I'm so thankful because he has blessed us both abundantly in our marriage."

The word *wounds* may be the most appropriate way to describe the emotional injuries suffered in a bad first marriage or from the death of a beloved spouse—especially if that death is premature. *Wounds* implies "scars," constant visible reminders of past pain and damage. But reminders of the past need not always be painful, nor do they have to bring to mind negative images. If you look, you can also find positive reminders of your past life, ones that you will come to cherish. And you can use these, too, to help build a healthy, loving, God-centered new life.

QUESTION:
Where can you find
encouragement
when life's storms
threaten to knock
you down?

FAMILY MEMORIAL STONES

Sometimes things will come into your life that will so wonderfully bless and amaze you that you will be certain they will remain forever at the forefront of your mind. Because of them, your gratitude to God will flow forever from your tongue. But somehow it never seems to happen that way. Other events occur in your life, and those wonderful blessings get pushed back. Other words take the place of the words of thanksgiving. You remember those blessed events, all right, but the joy begins to fade.

Before that happens, build yourself some memorial stones.

You do know about memorial stones, don't you? Listen to this one Kay has left from her first marriage: "In 1990, while our family was in Oxford, England, on our last vacation together, our house burned to the ground. Dan, who was then just a family friend, had called us in England to tell us about the fire, and he and his family had gone to the site to try to see if anything could be saved. They found nothing but a pile of rubble and ashes. When we got back I walked numbly through the wasteland, searching desperately for something I could hold in my hand, something from "before" that I could take with me and keep, something that would provide a tangible bridge between what was and the unknown that lay ahead of me. But Dan had been right; there was nothing left. And the bulldozer operators were waiting impatiently to clear the site.

"As I reluctantly made my way back through the ruins toward the street, I stubbed my toe against something in what had been the dining room. I stooped down and dug it out, then held it up and blew off the ashes. What I held in my hand looked like an honest-to-goodness piece of modern art. Its base was formed by a set of turkey-shaped salt and pepper-shakers, forever molded beak-to-beak by the crystal goblets that had melted over them. The shakers had been a gift from my sixth grade teacher who had always expressed such faith in me and my potential.

"On top of the turkeys was the melted base of a silver candlestick, a wedding gift to Larry and me. To one side were the melted remains of my grandmother's milk-glass sugar bowl, and on the other side was the delicate china cup I bought on our honeymoon. Balanced on one side was my daughter Lisa's baby spoon and fork, and on the other was my son Eric's long-handled baby spoon. The entire piece was cemented together and glazed over with a sparkling layer of melted glass and crystal.

"I had asked God for something I could hold in my hand. God gave me a summary of our family's life that I could carry with me forever!

"To this day that memorial sits on a special shelf in our china cabinet. Although it started as a Strom memorial stone, it has very much become a Kline-Strom memorial, for we can point to it as clear evidence of how God provided for us before we were even together.

But that's not our only memorial stone, nor our most important one. Dan also brought a memorial stone into our family. It is a plain blue King James Bible dated August 16, 1973, with "Daniel E. Kline" embossed in gold leaf on the front cover. It was a gift to Dan from a man named Max Perlman, long before Dan had ever opened a Bible or even cared to do so.

As Dan tells it, "As his temporary boss, I had recognized Max for his long and devoted efforts as a postal clerk, and along with the recognition came a cash award of about $200. I didn't know it at the time, but Max and his wife, both Christian Jews, were doing all they could to help keep their daughter in medical school. They'd already spent all they had and were praying for just this extra sum of money to meet a final, critical obligation. So to them this money was, literally, a godsend, and—at least in Max's mind—I was his instrument. In gratitude, Max gave me the most precious thing he could think of in return—a Bible.

I didn't know it then, but Max was the real "instrument of God," for that Bible and Max's promise that he would always pray for me was a turning point in my life, what I mark as the beginning of God's calling me to himself. That Bible is my memorial stone, of my salvation and of a wonderful man named Max Perlman, who touched my life only briefly but with everlasting consequence."

Do you have memorial stones? They are important for two reasons:

They Serve as Spiritual Markers for Your Family
Memorial stones are concrete reminders of what God has done for you in the past. When those tough times come, when troubles and trials assail and batter your marriage, and you are

tempted to question whether God cares for you at all, you can hold fast to one another and look to those tangible testaments of his power and grace. You can remind each other of the faithfulness he has shown you in the past and be encouraged.

They Serve as a Witness to Others

In Joshua 3, we read how God told Joshua to command the flooded waters of the Jordan River to pile up on one side so that the Israelites could safely cross over into Canaan on dry ground. Then Joshua instructed twelve strong men, one from each tribe, to go back out to the riverbed and each heft up a large stone (Joshua 4:5-7). They were to lug these out and pile them up together to make a huge memorial that anyone passing by could see for generations to come.

"When your children's children ask you what these stones mean," Joshua told the people, "you tell them what happened here today."

Whenever anyone sees our elegantly sculpted, crystal-encrusted piece of modern art and asks, "Hey, what's that?" we always say, "I'm so glad you asked! Let me tell you how God provided just what we needed in the most astounding way!"

When someone asks, "Max Perlman? Who's that?" we say, "Great question! Let me tell you a great story!"

Maureen has her marriage license framed because her very marriage is a memorial stone. "One of the important reasons my husband was first attracted to me was because I was a Christian," she says. "Although he wasn't practicing at the time, I'm sure that God had a plan and made us particularly attractive to one another. Because of some really bad experiences he had in his childhood congregation, James was extremely reluctant to become involved again in 'formal church worship,' but through God's grace he has put most of that behind him. I cannot tell you how much being able to worship and pray with my husband and raise our three children to love God has meant to us. It has been the strongest glue in our relationship."

And what about the trials and tribulations of life?

Just ask Janet and Peter. "It has taken twenty-two years of growing together and going through the fiery trials to get to a common ground," Janet says. "But we know for sure that God is the common thread that keeps a marriage together." Their memorial stone is their wedding album in which they place a new picture on each anniversary.

"That very first Hawaiian picture helps us remember first how God miraculously brought us two 'old folks' together, and second, God's faithfulness and the firm foundation on which our marriage is built. After all these years, it is for sure our marriage would have dissolved without the power of the Holy Spirit constantly bringing us back to his standard for love and commitment for marriage."

"And now these three remain: faith, hope and love. But the greatest of these is love" (1 Corinthians 13:13).

FOR DISCUSSION

Think together and see if you can pinpoint your own memorial stones:

- Are they displayed in places where they can remind you of God's working in your life?

- Are they in places where they will attract the attention of others?

Take some time to thank God for allowing you those times when his love and care felt especially close. Ask him to bring them to your mind in your times of need.

You and your partner both grow as you seek to know God better. Search the Scriptures together.

For richer or for poorer, in sickness and in health, and forsaking all others, until death us do part.

TRADITIONAL
WEDDING VOWS

Resources

Books

Burkett, Larry. *The Family Financial Workbook: A Practical Guide to Budgeting.* Chicago: Moody, 2000. Finances are one of the two leading causes of marriage breakup. This excellent financial workbook is a great tool for helping a family manage their money wisely and well.

Chapman, Gary. *The Five Languages of Love: How to Express Heartfelt Commitment to Your Mate.* Chicago: Northfield, 1992. Most people are generally aware that we all express love in different ways. But that doesn't mean we don't keep right on looking to receive love from our marriage partners the same way we give it, which leads to misunderstandings, quarrels, hurt feelings and worse. Chapman explains how understanding each other's love languages enables partners to give and receive love.

Cloud, Dr. Henry, and Dr. John Townsend. *Boundaries in Marriage.* Grand Rapids, Mich.: Zondervan, 1999. Many people who responded to our survey cited the difficulty of establishing where their personal boundaries should be drawn within their marriage. Cloud and Townsend address this crucial topic in this award-winning and biblically-based book. There also is a workbook available.

Gottman, John M., Ph.D., and Nan Silver. *The Seven Principles for Making Marriage Work.* New York: Three Rivers Press, 1999. This wonderfully practical marriage guide uses scientific procedures to guide couples toward successful, lasting relationships. It is loaded with questionnaires and exercises, and has all kinds of amazing results from years of research.

Harley, Willard F., Jr. *Fall in Love, Stay in Love.* Grand Rapids, Mich.: Revell, 2001. In this follow-up to *His Needs, Her Needs*, Harley shows couples how to stay in love by avoiding habits that chip away at each other. It is a helpful guide for achieving a lifetime of romantic, passionate love for each other.

———. *His Needs, Her Needs: Building an Affair-Proof Marriage.* Grand Rapids, Mich.: Revell, 1986. This book has been indispensable to us (Dan and Kay). Harley has discovered the astounding truth that marriage works only when each spouse takes the time to consider the other's needs, then takes the time to meet those needs. We highly recommend it.

O'Brien, Gene and Judith Tate. *Couples Praying: A Special Intimacy.* New York: Paulist, 1986. This is the only book we found specifically on praying together as a couple, and unfortunately it is out of print. There are a number of Internet sites such as Amazon.com where, as of this writing, a number of copies can be ordered for as little as $2.50 each.

Parrott, Dr. Leslie, and Dr. Les Parrott. *Saving Your Second Marriage Before It Starts.* Grand Rapids, Mich.: Zondervan, 2001. Written by husband and wife family therapists and a clinical psychologist, this book is designed for couples preparing for marriage who desperately want to beat the ominous remarriage failure rate of sixty percent. But it also can benefit newly married couples who fall into the remarriage category.

Reagan, Nancy, and Ronald Reagan. *I Love You, Ronnie.* New York: Bantam, 2000. From the time Ronald Reagan met Nancy Davis in 1950 until he was quieted by Alzheimer's disease in the 1990s, he wrote letters to his beloved. This book is a touching insight into the love story of a man who remarried at forty-one and just celebrated his fiftieth wedding anniversary.

Rosenau, Dr. Douglas E. *A Celebration of Sex.* Nashville, Tenn.: Thomas Nelson, 1994. The subtitle for this excellent book is "A Guide to Enjoying God's Gift of Married Sexual Pleasure." That largely sums up the book's purpose, but Dr. Rosenau's dedication is so well put we include part of it here as well: "To a wise and loving Creator, who graciously gave us the joy of marriage and making love. Thank you, Lord, for the intimate playfulness and bonding warmth of a sexual companionship."

Stark, Marg. *What No One Tells the Bride.* New York: MFJ Books, 1998. We were guided to this book by one of our survey respondents who wrote, "This book gave me lots of insights into married life for older singles. If you haven't read it, you should." We hadn't, so we did. Then we passed it along to several others who fit the category of older singles—especially in their thirties and forties—and they agreed that this book did a great job of addressing some of their concerns and reassuring them. Hence its inclusion here.

Stevens, R. Paul. *Marriage Spirituality: Ten Disciplines for Couples Who Love God.* Downers Grove, Ill.: InterVarsity Press, 1989. The author suggests using this book as the basis of a ten-week experiment in spiritual friendship as a couple. The book is out of print, but a lot of copies are floating around.

Strom, Kay Marshall, and Daniel E. Kline. *Hand in Hand: Devotions for the Later- (and Lately-) Married.* Ann Arbor, Mich.: Servant, 2003. It is because we strongly believe in the importance of couples having a time of biblical, prayerful meditation together that we wrote this book of sixty devotions and geared it specifically to couples who marry after the age of thirty-five.

Wisdom, Susan, and Jennifer Green. *Stepcoupling: Creating and Sustaining a Strong Marriage in Today's Blended Family.* New York: Three Rivers Press, 2002. Wisdom, who specializes in counseling stepfamilies, and Green provide tips and strategies for dealing with the issues remarried couples face with a wealth of advice from real-life step couples.

Websites

Focus on the Family
<www.family.org>

The website of Focus on the Family is packed with articles on a broad range of topics of interest to couples and families.

Grand Rapids, Michigan, Community Marriage Policy
<www.GGRCmarriagepolicy.org>

Although focused on Grand Rapids, Michigan, this great site has some wonderful resources and information for everyone. It's worth checking out.

Marriage Builders
<www.marriagebuilders.com>

In this website, Dr. Willard Harley introduces visitors to some of the best ways to overcome marital conflicts and restore love. There are articles, question-and-answer columns and other information on everything from communication to sexual problems, from finances to affection.

Marriage Savers
<www.marriagesavers.com>

"Prepare for life-long marriages, strengthen existing marriages, restore troubled marriages." Working through local churches, this nationwide effort recruits experienced couples to counsel younger marrieds. Interested in mentoring? Check them out.

Marriage Saving Ideas

<www.marriagesavingideas.com >

This site is something lightweight—a wee bit cutesy but also great fun.

National Marriage Encounter

<www.marriage-encounter.org >

Several of the couples who responded to our survey recommended Marriage Encounter. This group's stated goal is to "enable couples to discover God's vision of marriage and family life and spiritual diversity, thereby leading them to a clearer understanding of their relationship with each other and with God."

Smart Marriage: Coalition for Marriage, Family and Couples Education

<www.smartmarriages.com >

The coalition serves as a clearinghouse that will help people find the information they need to strengthen marriages and families. There are links to such topics as marriage, family and couples education. It is an independent, nonpartisan, nondenominational, nonsectarian organization. Their work is promoted entirely by the proceeds of the annual "Smart Marriages/Happy Families" conference. CMFCE produces a free e-newsletter.

Stepfamilies Association of America

<www.saafamilies.org >

<www.stepfam.org >

1-800-735-0329

Besides a great deal of helpful information, these comprehensive sites contain advocacy information, educational resources, a resource catalog and much more. An especially helpful feature is the section on book reviews, with each review followed by information on how to order that specific book.

Mastering Communications— in Marriage, in Work, in Relationships

Kay Strom and Dan Kline are available to speak to your church or group. In addition to keynotes and talks, they can also be booked for workshops or seminars on marriage and relationships, focusing especially on later-in-life marriages.

Kay began her writing career in 1980 and now has more than thirty books to her credit. Dan became a professional speaker in 1990 and has addressed numerous Fortune 500 companies as well as many smaller groups. Since marrying in 1998, they have been blending their skills and careers to better serve others, to better serve the Lord and to bring greater personal fulfillment and meaning to their lives.

Now partners in Kline, Strom & Associates, Kay and Dan speak at and lead seminars, retreats, conferences and special events throughout the country. Through God's guidance and their growing involvement in mission work, more and more of their speaking and Kay's writing is taking them to a variety of groups, cultures and nations around the world. Together they have spoken to well over 100,000 people in more than twenty countries.

If you would like to get in touch with Dan and Kay, you can contact them several ways:

3463 State Street No. 555
Santa Barbara, CA 93105
Phone: 1-805-964-2814
Fax: 1-805-967-7767
E-mail: kay@kaystrom.com
       dan@dankline.com
<www.kaystrom.com >
<www.dankline.com >